GOAT MATING GUIDE

"A Comprehensive Manual for Successful Breeding, Reproduction, and Health Management of Goats"

By

John William Bush (The Farmer's House)

Copyright@2024 John William Bush "The Farmer's House"

All rights reserved The publisher's permission is required before this book may be copied or reproduced in any way. As a result, nothing therein can be transmitted, saved electronically, or retained in a database. The original publisher's consent is required before any part or all of the material may be copied, scanned, faxed, or stored.

TABLE OF CONTENT

The Dancing of Nature: An Exploration into the World of Goat Mating 8

Introduction 13
  Welcome to the Breeding World of Goats 13
  The Value of Appropriate Mating Procedures in Goat Breeding... 15
  Knowing About Goat Procreation 18

Chapter 1: Introduction to Goat Breeding.................23
  Selecting the Best Breed for Your Requirements 23
  Organizing Your Program for Breeding 27
    Establishing a Breeding Timetable 27
    Breeding Procedures and Strategies 30
  Choosing Healthful Breeding Stock........................ 31

Chapter 2: Comprehending the Anatomy and Physiology of Goat Reproduction................................37
  The Reproductive System of Females....................37
    Female Reproductive System Anatomy 37
    The Female Reproductive System's Physiology 39
    Fertilization and Ovulation 41

Gestation and Pregnancy..................................44
The Reproductive System of Men....................48
   Control of Hormones and Sperm Production... 51
   Spermatogenesis..52
The Impact of Hormones on Reproduction...........57
Chapter 3: The Indication of Heat 61
   How to Spot Heat Signs in Female Goats 61
   Comprehending the Estrus Cycle.....................64
Chapter 4: Strategies and Methods for Breeding....71
   Natural or Organic Mating 71
   Artificial Insemination....................................74
   Selective Breeding and Line Breeding..............79
Chapter 5: Gestation and Pregnancy 85
   Verifying the Pregnancy 85
   Gestational Period and Handling 88
      Goat Gestation Period................................88
      Gestational Stages....................................89
   Typical Pregnancy Issues 92
Chapter 6: Birth and Kidding................................99
   Labor Signs in Female Goats..........................99
      Signs of Labor in Goats..............................99

Labor Stages in Goats 101
Helping with Challenging Births 103
Taking Care of Newborn Children 107
  Taking Care of Infants 111
  Medical Attention for Infants 112
Chapter 7: Handling Reproductive Health 113
Preventing and Treating Reproductive Disorders
.... 113
  Stopping Reproductive Issues 113
  Identifying the Symptoms of Reproductive
  Issues 115
Immunizations and Maintaining Health 117
  Typical Reproductive Illnesses 118
  Tips for Maintaining General Health 120
Consumption of Foods for Reproductive Health 121
  The Dietary Needs of Goat Breeding 122
  Feeding and Nutrition Management for Healthy
  Reproduction 123
Chapter 8: Breeding for Specific Goals 125
  Breeding to Produce Milk 125
  Breeding for High-Quality Meat 129
  Breeding for Display or Exhibition 133

Chapter 9: Maintaining Records and Managing Breeding Programs 139

Importance of Record Keeping 139
Kinds of Documents to Maintain 140
Best Practices for Maintaining Records and Managing Breeding Programs 141

Establishing a Breeding Timetable 143

Assessing the Success of Breeding Programs . 146

Chapter 10: Breeding Stock Sales & Marketing 151

Promoting Your Breeding Stock 151
Techniques for Marketing Breeding Stock 151
Outlets for Breeding Stock Sales 152
The Best Ways to Promote and Sell Breeding Stock 153

Pricing and Sales Negotiation 155
Determining Breeding Stock Prices 155
Sales negotiations with purchasers 156
Managing Successful Pricing Strategies 157

Sustaining Connections with Purchasers 158
Techniques of Communication 159
Customer Service Procedures 160
After-Sale Assistance 160

Chapter 11: Legal and Ethical Aspects of Goat Breeding 163

Welfare of Animals and Breeding Procedures .. 163

Standards for Animal Welfare 163

Respect for the Laws and Regulations 164

Regulations Governing the Breeding and Sale of Goats 165

Breeding Goats' Effects on the Environment 167

In summary 171

Benefits and Difficulties of Breeding Goats 171

Benefits of Breeding Goats: 171

Obstacles in Goat Breeding: 172

Closing Remarks and Inspiration 174

Appendices 176

Glossary of Terms 176

Sample Breeding Records 179

The Dancing of Nature: An Exploration into the World of Goat Mating

There is a timeless dance taking place in the gently undulating hills of a charming rural area, where the sun is kissing the ground and soft breezes are whispering through the trees. This dance is a celebration of life, nature, and future generations. Goats are the focal point of this dance because they are graceful, resilient animals whose reproductive cycles and mating rituals have been deeply ingrained in rural life.

As we go out on this exploration of goat mating, picture yourself in the middle of a vivid field, surrounded by inquisitive eyes and agile hooves. A new chapter in the natural cycle is announced by the gentle bleating of goats filling the air, creating a symphony of life.

Recognizing the critical significance of appropriate mating behaviors is the first step on our path. Goat rearing has long been a vital component of sustainable agriculture and means of subsistence. It involves more than just matching up two goats; it involves carefully planning the combination of features, genetics, and health to guarantee the health and output of subsequent generations.

Meet the keepers of this dance, the farmers, breeders, and caregivers whose expertise and enthusiasm determine the future of goat herds, as the first light of day falls on them. They'll walk us through the difficult process of choosing the best breed for a given need, such as milk yield, meat quality, or even exhibits.

Goat reproductive anatomy and physiology's hidden treasures get revealed as we dig deeper. Discover the complexities of the female reproductive system with us. It is a wonder of natural design that allows for the miracle of birth. Travel with the male goats, whose strength and vitality are essential for a good mating experience and healthy progeny.

The symphony of hormonal oscillations known as the estrus cycle, which signals the preparation for mating, is matched by the rhythm of nature. Master the art of timing in goat breeding by learning to recognize these subtle indications, which can range from behavioral changes to physical symptoms.

From the natural elegance of mating rituals to the accuracy of artificial insemination, breeding methods and techniques are the delicate moves of this dance. Learn the subtleties of selective breeding, where every combination has the power to influence the features and qualities that goat herds will bear in the future.

We see the wonder of pregnancy and gestation as the seasons change and new life emerges. Uncover the intricacies of goat birthing—the happy times of kidding and the possible difficulties—by following the path of doe-bears as they nourish life within.

The dance of nature is not without its challenges, though. Investigate the field of reproductive health management, where proactive approaches and close monitoring ensure the welfare of breeding goats. Every facet—from disease prevention and treatment to ensuring ideal nutrition—contributes to the success of a breeding program.

Goat breeding involves a careful balancing act between experience, intuition, and knowledge, making it both an art and a science. Breeding decisions have an impact on future generations, whether your objective is to increase milk yield, boost meat quality, or just maintain heritage breeds.

We explore record-keeping, breeding program administration, and ethical issues as our voyage progresses. Explore the ethical terrain of animal welfare, regulatory compliance, and environmental sustainability. Learn how data can guide breeding decisions.

The market, a thriving center where breeding stock finds new homes and relationships are formed, is where our investigation culminates. Discover the skill of selling your goats, determining reasonable prices, and fostering enduring connections with purchasers who are as passionate about sustainable agriculture as you are.

Every strand in the vast fabric of nature is essential. The intricate bonds that bind us to the land, the animals, and the eternal rhythm of life itself are demonstrated by our voyage through the realm of goat mating.

Come along on a journey of exploration, care, and respect for the dance of nature as we uncover the mysteries, revel in the pleasures, and face the difficulties of goat breeding. Greetings and salutations, and welcome to the Goat Mating Guide, where each page promises fresh starts and the inheritance of previous generations.

May your footsteps in this dance echo with the harmony of nature's symphony, and may your journey be filled with the richness of knowledge, passion, and respect for the timeless art of goat mating.

GOAT MATING GUIDE   John William Bush (The Farmer's House)

GOAT MATING GUIDE   John William Bush (The Farmer's House)

Introduction

Welcome to the Breeding World of Goats

AN EXPLORATION OF SUSTAINABLE AGRICULTURE'S CORE

Greetings from the dynamic world of goat raising, where innovation and tradition coexist and existence is determined by the cycles of the natural world. As you go out on your adventure, get ready to become entangled in a web of wisdom, fervor, and age-old customs that have supported societies for countless years.

Raising goats is more than just a means of subsistence; it's a way of life with a deep connection to the land, the animals, and the natural cycles. There's a balance, a harmony that touches the very core of sustainable agriculture in the verdant valleys and rolling hills where goats wander.

The skill of matching two goats together is a deliberate and thorough procedure that calls for in-depth knowledge, meticulous planning, and a keen eye for detail. This basic yet profound reality is at the core of goat breeding. New life, new qualities, and new prospects for both the herd and the breeder are promised by every mating.

You'll learn that the world of goat breeding is a journey of discovery as you learn more about it; a trip that reveals the secrets of animal husbandry, the wonders of nature, and the mysteries of life. Every facet of goat breeding, from the choice of breeding stock to the maintenance of reproductive health, bears witness to the resourcefulness and tenacity of those who engage in it.

You will take a thorough look into goat breeding in the pages that follow, covering everything from the fundamentals of choosing the best breed to the intricacies of running an effective breeding operation. You will come across breeders, farmers, and caregivers who have devoted their lives to the art and science of goat breeding along the route; everyone has a lot of knowledge to impart as well as a special tale to tell.

You will learn to understand the close bond that exists between people and animals as well as the significant influence that sustainable agriculture can have on the state of the environment and the welfare of future generations as you immerse yourself in the world of goat rearing. These pages include ideas and advice that will inspire, educate, and empower you to achieve greater success in your goat breeding pursuits, regardless of your experience level.

I so extend an invitation to you, my dear reader, to enter the field of goat breeding with an open mind and an open heart. Let yourself be enthralled by the natural beauty, the goat's tenacity, and the ageless customs that have kept villages alive for ages. Greetings from the world of goat breeding, where each day is a fresh start and each goat holds the potential to be a better future.

The Value of Appropriate Mating Procedures in Goat Breeding

MAKING CERTAIN YOUR HERD IS HEALTHY, PRODUCTIVE, AND SUSTAINABLE

It is impossible to exaggerate the significance of appropriate mating techniques among the undulating hills and lush meadows where goats wander. Goat rearing has long been a pillar of sustainable agriculture, giving communities all over the world access to milk, meat, and company. The meticulous planning of mating, which determines the destiny of goat herds and guarantees their sustainability, productivity, and health, is the essential component of this activity.

For goat populations to remain vibrant and genetically diverse, proper mating habits are crucial. The foundation of contemporary goat breeding is selective breeding, which gives breeders the ability to select features that improve temperament, productivity, and health. Breeders can lower the danger of genetic problems and increase the overall quality of their herds by choosing healthy, genetically varied breeding stock.

Furthermore, preserving each goat's health and well-being depends on appropriate mating procedures. Inadequate mating can cause injury or even death, and breeding too early or too late might cause problems during pregnancy and labor. Breeders can limit health risks and protect the well-being of their goats by careful timing and supervising mating.

Optimizing the fertility of goat herds also requires proper mating methods. Breeders can maximize the quantity and quality of offspring produced by carefully choosing breeding pairings and timing matings. In addition to making goat farming more profitable, this guarantees a steady supply of food for communities worldwide.

Appropriate mating techniques are crucial for maintaining the heritage and cultural relevance of goat breeds, in addition to their health and productivity. Urbanization and contemporary farming methods are putting several traditional goat breeds in danger of going extinct. Breeders can contribute to the preservation of these breeds' distinctive genetic characteristics and cultural history for future generations by carefully choosing breeding pairings and highlighting their worth.

Appropriate mating methods have benefits that go beyond the farm gate. Breeders can help ensure food security, rural development, and environmental sustainability by keeping healthy, productive goat herds. Because of their adaptability to a wide range of conditions, goats can flourish in marginal areas where other livestock might struggle. Breeders can contribute to the improvement of soil fertility, prevention of erosion, and promotion of biodiversity in these places by encouraging sustainable goat breeding methods.

Appropriate mating behaviors are not only scientifically justified; they also reflect morality and accountability. The privilege of breeding animals entails a responsibility to protect their welfare and well-being. Breeders can contribute to a better public perception of the livestock sector and show their dedication to animal welfare by encouraging ethical breeding practices.

In conclusion, it is impossible to exaggerate the significance of appropriate mating techniques in goat breeding. Appropriate mating procedures are critical to the long-term viability of goat farming, as they protect genetic diversity and cultural heritage while also guaranteeing the health and production of herds. Breeders may contribute to a better future for goats, farmers, and communities worldwide by encouraging ethical breeding techniques.

Knowing About Goat Procreation

We shall provide a thorough Overview of the complexities of goat breeding and reproductive biology here. The fascinating and complex process of goat reproduction is controlled by various biological systems that guarantee the survival of the species. We learn more about the reproductive anatomy and physiology of goats as we explore their world of reproduction. This helps us to understand these amazing animals better and their significance for global sustainable agriculture and lifestyles.

The female reproductive system, a wonder of biological engineering created to support and nurture new life, is the center of goat reproduction. The ovary releases an egg and the uterus gets ready for pregnancy at the end of a beautifully choreographed dance of hormones and physiological changes called the estrous cycle in female goats.

The proestrus, estrus, metestrus, and diestrus are the four phases of the estrous cycle. The cycle starts with proestrus, which is defined by the growth of ovarian follicles and an increase in estrogen levels. The period known as estrus, or "heat," is when ovulation takes place and the female is ready for mating. The development of the corpus luteum, a transient endocrine tissue that secretes progesterone, marks the transitional stage known as menstruation. The last phase of the cycle, known as the diestrus, occurs when the corpus luteum regresses in the absence of fertilization.

The estrous cycle lasts between 18 and 24 days, though it varies according on the breed and individual goat. Since the female is only fertile at this period, detecting estrus is essential to a good mating experience. Restlessness, frequent urination, mounting activity, and a swollen vulva are all indicators that a goat is in estrus.

Bucks, or male goats, are essential to the reproductive process. The male reproductive system is made to produce and transmit sperm—male gametes that fertilize female eggs—as efficiently as possible. The scrotum contains the testes, which are responsible for the process of spermatogenesis, which creates sperm. The epididymis, a coiled tube behind the testes, is where sperm are kept until they are released during ejaculation into the urethra.

The breeding season is when bucks show seasonal variations in their reproductive activity. While some breeds may breed all year round, in temperate areas the breeding season usually begins in the fall. Bucks have elevated testosterone levels during breeding season, which promotes sperm maturation and production.

Goat mating behavior is a complicated combination of social dynamics, hormone cues, and instinct. A range of vocalizations, body positions, and scent-marking techniques are employed by bucks to entice females and assert their dominance in the herd. When a female denotes that she is in estrus, the male will attempt to copulate with her, frequently vocalizing and acting aggressively to scare off potential partners.

Following a successful mating process, sperm fertilize the egg, creating a zygote, a single-cell embryo that will eventually grow into a new goat. As the zygote passes through the fallopian tube and implants itself in the uterine lining, it goes through a sequence of cell divisions that will continue to shape its development for the period of gestation.

Goats typically go through 150 days of gestation, though this might vary based on breed, diet, and environmental factors. The placenta is a specialized organ that develops in the uterus and provides the growing child with nutrition and oxygen from the mother during gestation.

A pregnant doe nearing the conclusion of her gestation will display a range of physical and behavioral changes that signal the impending process of kidding or giving birth. These symptoms include a swelling udder, restlessness, and nesting behavior. The process of kidding is normal and usually goes unproblematic, though occasionally help may be needed.

The newborn child depends on its mother's milk for protection and sustenance after kidding. Goat milk is nutrient- and antibody-rich, supporting the child's growth and development. Mothers and children have a close relationship, and mothers will look out for and shield their children until they are mature enough to take care of themselves.

Comprehending the process of goat reproduction is vital for proficient goat breeding and handling. Breeders may ensure the health and vitality of their herds for future generations by making informed decisions about breeding procedures, nutrition, and health treatment by obtaining an understanding of the complexities of their reproductive biology.

GOAT MATING GUIDE   John William Bush (The Farmer's House)

Chapter 1: Introduction to Goat Breeding

Selecting the Best Breed for Your Requirements

Selecting the appropriate breed is an essential first step in developing a productive and long-lasting breeding program for goats. Size, temperament, milk output, and meat quality are just a few of the distinctive qualities that set each breed apart, so it's critical to carefully weigh your needs and goals before choosing one. This chapter will discuss the many aspects to take into account when selecting a breed of goat, along with some of the most well-liked varieties for varied uses.

CONSIDERATIONS FOR SELECTING A BREED OF GOAT

Before selecting a goat breed, you should think about several crucial elements that will affect how well your breeding program performs. Among these are:

1. Purpose: The primary factor to take into account when selecting a breed of goat is the reason you want to herd goats. Do you want to raise meat goats for meat production, dairy goats for milk, or fiber goats for wool? Since every breed has a distinct purpose, it's critical to select a breed that complements your objectives.

2. *Climate and Environment:* Goats are versatile animals that can live in many different types of climates, however, some varieties do better in particular regions than others. When selecting a breed, take into account the climate and surroundings of your area since this will affect the health, output, and general well-being of the animal.

3. *Space and Housing:* The needs for space and housing vary throughout goat breeds. While certain kinds do well in settings where they are allowed to roam freely, others are better suited to strict confinement and supervision. When selecting a breed, take into account the available space and the kind of housing.

4. *Temperament:* If you are new to maintaining goats, the temperament of the breed is crucial to take into account. While some varieties can be more aggressive or high-strung, others are renowned for their docile demeanor and ease of handling.

5. *Breeding Stock Availability:* Take into account the availability of breeding stock in your area before selecting a breed. Certain breeds could be more accessible and common, while others might be harder to find and rarer.

POPULAR BREEDS OF GOATS FOR VARIOUS USES

There are numerous goat breeds to select from, each with special qualities and benefits of their own. For various uses, the following are some of the most well-liked goat breeds:

1. DAIRY GOATS: Known for their nutritious, high-quality milk, dairy goats are developed specifically to produce large amounts of milk. Popular breeds of dairy goats include:

- ✓ **Nubian:** Nubian goats are noted for producing milk with a high butterfat content, which is perfect for creating cheese and butter. Their friendly nature and their long, floppy ears are other well-known attributes.
- ✓ **Saanen:** Known for their great milk production, Saanen goats are one of the biggest breeds of dairy goats. Their demeanor is kind and quiet, and they are usually entirely white.
- ✓ **Alpine:** Known for their high milk production and ability to adapt to many conditions, alpine goats are a versatile breed. They have a range of colors and are renowned for being gregarious and extroverted.

2. MEAT GOATS: Known for their quick growth rates and premium meat, meat goats are developed specifically to produce meat. Popular breeds of meat goats include:

- ✓ **Boer:** Boer goats are a big, meaty breed distinguished by their quick development and excellent feed efficiency. They are recognized for their submissive demeanor and are usually white with a reddish.
- ✓ **Kiko:** Hardy meat goats with a reputation for thriving in challenging conditions are the Kiko breed. They have outstanding meat quality and are usually white or cream in color.
- ✓ **Spanish:** Known for their versatility and resilience, Spanish goats are a sturdy breed. They are well-known for their superior meat quality and mothering skills, and they are available in a range of hues.

3. FIBER GOATS:

Wool from these goats is bred specifically to be utilized in a wide range of fabrics. Popular breeds of fiber goats include:

- ✓ **Angora:** Angora goats are renowned for its soft and shiny mohair fiber, which is considered to be exquisite. They are renowned for their mild disposition and are usually white.
- ✓ **Cashmere:** Fine cashmere goat wool, valued for its warmth and tenderness, is the reason cashmere goats are raised. They are renowned for being resilient and are usually white or gray in color.
- ✓ **Pygora:** Bred for their silky, opulent fiber, Pygora goats are a mix between Angora and Pygmy goats.

They are recognized for their amiable and lively dispositions and come in an array of hues.

In order to establish a productive and long-lasting goat breeding operation, selecting the appropriate breed is essential. You can choose a breed that is ideal for your purposes and will flourish in your setting by carefully weighing your objectives, your demands, and the distinctive qualities of each breed. There is a goat breed out there for everyone, regardless of their interests in producing dairy, meat, or fiber.

Organizing Your Program for Breeding

A good breeding program for goats needs to be carefully planned, meticulously executed, and devoted to the long-term health and welfare of your herd. We will go over the crucial actions you need to do to set up your breeding program in this chapter, including choosing breeding stock, putting together a breeding plan, and keeping track of breeding records.

Establishing a Breeding Timetable

Making a breeding schedule is the next step after choosing your breeding stock. To guarantee a consistent supply of offspring all year long, you can plan and manage the timing of matings with the use of a breeding schedule.

Some things to think about while planning a breeding program are:

BREEDING SEASON: Based on your goats' natural reproductive cycles and the local climate, ascertain when the best time to breed them is. While certain breeds can only reproduce during designated seasons, others might be bred all year round.

ESTROUS CYCLE: Recognize when it is ideal to breed your goats based on their estrous cycle. The estrous phase, or heat, lasts one to three days in the majority of goats' 21-day cycle.

MATING TECHNIQUES: Choose between artificial insemination (AI) and natural mating for breeding. The most popular technique, known as natural mating, entails letting bucks and does mate spontaneously. Without a male goat on the farm, does with desired genetics can be bred using AI.

KEEPING TRACK OF BREEDING RECORDS

Maintaining thorough breeding records is crucial to monitoring your herd's performance and ancestry. Records pertaining to breeding should contain details like:

DAY OF MATING: To keep track of the timing of pregnancies and kidding, note the day on which each doe is bred.

SIRE INFORMATION: To trace the lineage of offspring, note the name and identifying number of the buck used for mating.

PREGNANCY CHECKS: Keep track of the outcomes of these tests in order to track the development of pregnancies and spot any possible problems.

KIDDING RECORDS: To monitor the well-being and output of your herd, keep track of the date of kidding, the number of babies born, and any issues that arose.

PEDIGREE DATA: To trace the genetic background and ancestry of your goat herd, keep thorough pedigree data for every goat.

You may make well-informed decisions about mating pairs, keep an eye on the production and general health of your herd, and follow the progress of individual goats over time by maintaining thorough breeding records.

Breeding Procedures and Strategies

To increase your herd's productivity and genetic makeup, you can employ a variety of breeding strategies. Typical breeding techniques include the following:

- ✓ **Natural mating:** Using controlled breeding facilities or pasture breeding to allow bucks and does to mate naturally.
- ✓ **Artificial insemination (AI):** The process of inseminating a doe with fresh or frozen semen from a male goat. Breeders no longer need to maintain a male goat on the farm in order to get DNA from distant or superior bucks thanks to AI.
- ✓ **Embryo transfer:** To maximize the number of progeny from a single mating, embryos from a genetically superior doe are collected and transferred to the recipient does.
- ✓ **Selective breeding:** Breeding animals with desired qualities in order to improve those traits in subsequent generations is known as selective breeding. It is possible to enhance desirable traits like meat quality, milk production, or other traits through selective breeding.

It's critical to carefully assess which breeding method best fits your aims and available resources because each has benefits and drawbacks.

A good breeding program for goats needs to be carefully planned, meticulously executed, and devoted to the long-term health and welfare of your herd. You can make sure that your breeding program is successful and that your herd is healthy and productive for many years to come by choosing the best breeding stock, planning a breeding schedule, keeping track of breeding records, and employing the proper breeding procedures and techniques.

Choosing Healthful Breeding Stock

Any goat breeding program's success depends on choosing healthy breeding stock. In addition to giving birth to better progeny, robust goats also enhance the general well-being and vigor of the herd. We will examine the most important aspects to take into account when choosing breeding stock in this thorough guide, including structural features, genetic factors, and health evaluations.

EVALUATIONS OF HEALTH

To make sure the goats are free from illness and genetic diseases, comprehensive health assessments must be performed before choosing breeding stock. Here are some important health evaluations to think about:

- ✓ **Physical checkup:** Give each goat a comprehensive physical checkup, noting any injuries or illnesses, calculating their body condition score, and analyzing their overall conformation.
- ✓ **Fecal Testing:** Examine fecal samples for internal parasites, as these might have a detrimental effect on the goats' well-being and output.
- ✓ **Blood Testing:** To make sure the goats are clear of infectious diseases like Johnes disease, CAE (Caprine Arthritis Encephalitis), and CL (Caseous Lymphadenitis), think about having blood tests.
- ✓ **Vaccination History:** Verify that the goats have received the most recent shots, including those for rabies, tetanus, and Clostridium perfringens.

GENETIC POINTS TO CONSIDER

Health, production, and conformation are all heavily influenced by genetics in goats. The following genetic factors should be taken into account when choosing breeding stock:

- ✓ **Pedigree:** Examine each goat's pedigree to evaluate their genetic heritage and ascertain whether or not they originate from robust and fruitful breeds.
- ✓ **Genetic Testing:** To check for inherited illnesses or characteristics that might be present in the breed, think about genetic testing. Genetic illnesses can be

identified by testing, which can also stop the disorders from being passed on to progeny.
- ✓ **Breeding Objectives:** When choosing breeding stock, take your breeding objectives into account. Choose goats that have the qualities that are most important to you, such as conformation, meat quality, or milk output.

TRAITS OF CONFORMATION

Conformational features pertain to the physical attributes of goats, encompassing their dimensions, form, and composition. The following conformational traits should be taken into account while choosing breeding stock:

1. Body Condition Score: Goats with a reasonable body condition score—that is, neither too skinny nor too fat—are better nourished and have good general health.

2. Structural Soundness: Select goats that exhibit good structural integrity, such as robust, well-built bodies, straight legs, and sound feet.

3. Udder Conformation (dairy goats): Choose does that have symmetrical, well-attached udders that are easy to milk and devoid of flaws or anomalies.

4. Horns: Take into consideration if you want polled (hornless) goats or goats with horns. Goats with horns may demand more care and may be more dangerous.

5. Coat Color and Pattern: Although coat color and pattern are mostly decorative factors, they can also reveal genetic diversity and purity in a breed.

BREEDING TECHNIQUES

To meet your breeding objectives, you must create a breeding strategy after you have chosen a healthy breeding stock. Think about the subsequent breeding tactics:

1. LINE BREEDING: The practice of breeding goats with similar bloodlines to preserve desired traits. While it might help correct good qualities, line breeding also raises the possibility of genetic problems.

2. OUTCROSSING: Creating new genetic material and boosting genetic variety through the breeding of unrelated goats. Although outcrossing can increase vitality and general health, it can also produce offspring with inconsistent features.

3. CROSSBREEDING: The process of breeding goats from two different breeds to blend the best features from each. Although hybrid vigor can be produced by crossbreeding, unforeseen features may arise.

4. SELECTION INTENSITY: Choosing only the finest individuals to breed to raise the herd's general caliber. While selection intensity may lessen genetic variety, it can aid in improving productivity and conformation.

5. BREEDING SEASON: Choose the best time to breed goats depending on local environment and the animals' natural reproductive cycles. The timing of pregnancies and kidding might be influenced by the breeding season.

Any goat breeding program's success depends on choosing healthy breeding stock. You can make sure that your breeding stock is robust, healthy, and genetically diversified by carrying out in-depth health examinations, taking conformational features and genetic factors into account, and creating a breeding plan. You may create a herd of goats that is robust and sustainable for future generations, in addition to being healthy and productive, with careful selection and management.

Chapter 2: Comprehending the Anatomy and Physiology of Goat Reproduction

The Reproductive System of Females

Goats' female reproductive systems are marvels of biological engineering, perfectly designed to aid in reproduction. A thorough understanding of the female reproductive system's anatomy and function is essential for productive goat breeding. The complex architecture and operations of the female reproductive system, from the ovaries to the uterus, as well as the hormonal regulation that controls the reproductive cycle, will all be covered in this chapter.

Female Reproductive System Anatomy

Goats' female reproductive systems are made up of a number of essential structures, each with a specific role in the reproduction process. Among these structures are:

1. Ovaries: The main reproductive organs of female goats, the ovaries are in charge of creating progesterone and estrogen as well as eggs, or oocytes. The ovary is situated in the abdominal cavity close to the kidneys and is about the size of an almond.

2. Oviducts: The oviducts, often called fallopian tubes, are thin tubes that connect the ovaries and uterus. The oviducts are in charge of moving eggs from the ovaries into the uterus and acting as a location for fertilization.

3. Uterus: The uterus is a pear-shaped organ that lies between the rectum and the bladder in the abdominal cavity. It is separated into two horns, each of which has an oviduct connection. During pregnancy, the uterus is in charge of providing the growing fetus with nourishment and support.

4. Cervix: A muscular structure at the uterine opening, the cervix aids in sealing the uterus during pregnancy and preventing pathogen access. The cervix relaxes to allow sperm to enter the uterus during estrus, or heat.

5. Vagina: The muscular tube that connects the cervix to the exterior of the body is called the vagina. It acts as the birth canal during kidding and as a passageway for sperm during mating.

The Female Reproductive System's Physiology

Hormones that govern the estrous cycle and pregnancy interact intricately to govern the female reproductive system in goats. The following are the main hormones that affect the female reproductive system:

1. Follicle-Stimulating Hormone (FSH): The anterior pituitary gland secretes follicle-stimulating hormone (FSH), which promotes the creation and expansion of ovarian follicles, which house the eggs.

2. luteinizing hormone (LH): The anterior pituitary gland also secretes luteinizing hormone (LH), which is responsible for initiating ovulation, or the release of a developed egg from the ovary.

3. Estrogen: Mainly produced by the ovaries, estrogen is in charge of the uterus's preparation for pregnancy as well as the development of secondary sexual characteristics.

4. Progesterone: Progesterone is a crucial hormone for preserving pregnancy and priming the uterus for embryo implantation. It is produced by the corpus luteum, a transitory endocrine tissue that forms following ovulation.

A LOOK AT BREEDING MANAGEMENT

A thorough understanding of the female reproductive system's anatomy and physiology is necessary for effective breeding management. Breeders can apply this understanding to:

- ✓ **Identify Estrus:** Breeders can tell when females are in heat and ready for mating by looking for behavioral and physical indicators of estrus, such as restlessness, frequent urination, and a swelling vulva.
- ✓ **Time Breeding:** By knowing when the estrous cycle occurs, breeders can plan matings to increase the likelihood of a successful fertilization and subsequent pregnancy.
- ✓ **Handle Pregnancy:** After a pregnancy has been confirmed, breeders can keep an eye on its development and get ready for kidding by giving the baby the right food and attention.
- ✓ **Prevent and Treat Reproductive Disorders:** By understanding the female reproductive system, breeders can recognize and treat conditions that may compromise fertility and reproductive efficiency.

The intricate and well-tuned female reproductive system in goats is vital to the reproduction process. Breeders can efficiently oversee breeding plans, optimize reproductive efficiency, and guarantee the health and welfare of their herds by having a thorough understanding of the anatomy and physiology of the female reproductive system.

Fertilization and Ovulation

Crucial steps in the goat reproductive cycle are ovulation and fertilization, which result in the development of a zygote and the onset of pregnancy. We'll look at the phases of ovulation and fertilization and the variables that can affect them.

THE OVULATION PROCESS

The process through which a developed egg, or oocyte, is expelled from the ovary and prepared for fertilization is known as ovulation. A spike in the pituitary gland's production of luteinizing hormone (LH) leads the mature follicle to burst and release the egg, initiating ovulation in goats. Usually, ovulation happens 24–36 hours following the LH spike.

Goat ovulation can be impacted by a number of variables, such as:

1. **PHOTOPERIOD:** Goats' ovulation timing is influenced by the duration of daylight, with longer days promoting earlier ovulation.

2. NUTRITION: Sufficient food intake is necessary for ovulation and healthy ovarian function. Ovulation might be irregular or delayed as a result of poor nutrition.

3. BREED AND AGE: Ovulation patterns might differ throughout goat breeds and age groups. Certain breeds and younger goats may ovulate more frequently or in greater quantities.

4. STRESS: Goats' ovulation can be interfered with by environmental stressors as transportation, overpopulation, and subpar shelter.

FERTILIZATION

The process via which a sperm cell enters an egg and unites with its nucleus to generate a zygote is known as fertilization. Fertilization usually takes place in the fallopian tubes of goats, where the sperm and egg converge. The sperm cells can survive for up to 48 hours in the fallopian tubes after passing past the cervix and into the uterus.

Several factors affect the process of fertilization in goats, such as:

Sperm Quality and Quantity: A sperm cell's capacity to fertilize an egg can be influenced by both its quality and quantity. The likelihood of successfully fertilizing an egg is higher in healthy, motile sperm cells.

Timing of Mating: Since the egg is only viable for a brief time after ovulation, timing is essential for effective fertilization. To increase the likelihood of conception, mating should take place around ovulation.

Sperm Transport: An essential part of fertilization is the movement of sperm cells from the cervix to the fallopian tubes. The likelihood of a successful fertilization can be decreased by any anomalies or disturbances in this process.

Uterine Environment: The uterine environment is important for fertilization because it must create an environment that allows sperm to survive and go to the fallopian tubes.

The zygote starts to split and grow as it passes through the fallopian tube and into the uterus following fertilization. The zygote implants itself into the uterine lining upon reaching the uterus, where it will proceed to develop into a fetus.

Goat reproduction depends on the intricate processes of ovulation and fertilization. It is essential to comprehend these mechanisms and the variables that may affect them in order to carry out successful breeding and reproduction. Breeders can increase their herds' chances of successful ovulation, fertilization, and pregnancy by managing them well and providing ideal conditions.

Gestation and Pregnancy

Crucial times in a goat's life cycle, pregnancy and gestation signal the start of a new life and the survival of the species. We will discuss the phases of pregnancy, the fetus's growth, and the care needed to ensure the health and wellbeing of the mother and her offspring throughout the gestation period.

Confirmation of Pregnancy

Goats are difficult to confirm pregnant since in the early stages of pregnancy there are no outward indicators of pregnancy. Nonetheless, there are a few ways to verify a pregnancy:

- ✓ **Ultrasound:** As early as 30 days after mating, ultrasound is a non-invasive technique that can be used to see the fetus and confirm pregnancy.
- ✓ **Blood Test:** Pregnancy-associated glycoproteins (PAGs), among other pregnancy-specific hormones, can be found using blood testing, which can be used to confirm pregnancy.
- ✓ **bodily Symptoms:** As a pregnancy develops, bodily symptoms including enlarged abdomens, developing udders, and altered behavior may be indicators.

Gestational period

A goat's gestation cycle lasts roughly 150 days, though it might vary somewhat based on breed, nutrition, and environmental circumstances. Three phases comprise gestation:

- ✓ **Early Gestation (Days 1–50):** The fertilized egg inserts itself in the uterine lining and starts to develop into an embryo during this phase of gestation. In addition, the placenta starts to develop, supplying the growing embryo with nutrition.
- ✓ **Mid gestation (Days 51–100):** At this point in the pregnancy, the embryo has grown into a fetus and the main bodily systems and organs are beginning to take shape. During this phase, the fetus grows quickly, and the mother may start to exhibit physical symptoms of pregnancy.
- ✓ **Days 101–150 of Late Gestation:** During the last phases of pregnancy, the fetus continues to grow and develop. Along with positioning itself for delivery, the fetus starts to face the birth canal.

Taking Care During Gestation

The health and welfare of the mother and her offspring depend on proper gestational care. The following are some essential elements of prenatal care:

1. NUTRITION: To promote the health of the mother and the development of the fetus, offer a balanced diet high in vitamins, minerals, and other nutrients. Depending on the dam's nutritional requirements and the gestational stage, modify the diet as necessary.

2. HOUSING: Give the dam a tidy, cozy, and well-ventilated space to rest and build a nest. Make sure there are no drafts, moisture issues, or other environmental stresses in the housing.

3. MONITORING: Keep a regular eye out for any indications of disease, discomfort, or issues with the dam. Make sure she is healthy and doing well by keeping an eye on her weight, appetite, and demeanor.

4. VACCINATIONS AND DEWORMING: To avoid infections and diseases that could affect her or the fetus, make sure the dam is up to date on her vaccinations and deworming.

5. EXERCISE: To encourage excellent health and prevent obesity, give the dam regular, mild exercise. Steer clear of hobbies or intense activity that could lead to stress or injury.

6. GETTING READY FOR KIDDING: As the deadline draws near, set up a spotless, private, and quiet space for joking. Give the dam all the supplies and bedding she will need to give birth.

KIDDING

Goats naturally and instinctively give birth to their young. This procedure is known as kidding. Usually, the dam will give birth to one or more children, though certain strains frequently produce twins or triplets. Three stages can be distinguished in kidding:

STAGE ONE: As the cervix dilates, the doe may show symptoms of restlessness, nesting behavior, and abdominal contractions during the first stage of labor.

STAGE TWO: The actual birthing process, in which the children are born, takes place during the second stage of labor. When each baby is delivered, usually head first, the doe will strain and push.

STAGE THREE: The placenta, or afterbirth, is expelled during the third stage of labor. Usually, the placenta contains vital nutrients and aids in stimulating milk production, so the doe will consume it.

Following kidding, it's critical to keep a careful eye out for any indications of disease or difficulties in the dam and the children. Give the dam plenty clean water, wholesome food, and a warm, dry place to recuperate from kidding.

A goat's pregnancy and gestation are crucial life phases that signify the start of a new life and the survival of the species. In order to protect the health and welfare of the mother and her offspring, proper management and care must be provided during the gestation period. You can contribute to a successful pregnancy and a robust, healthy herd of goats by giving sufficient nourishment, housing, supervision, and veterinary treatment.

The Reproductive System of Men

A marvel of biological engineering, the male reproductive system in goats is precisely designed to generate and distribute sperm for fertilization. The complex internal and external structures, as well as the hormone regulation and sperm generation and delivery procedures, of the male goat reproductive system will all be covered now.

EXTERNAL ORGANS

The penis, scrotum, testes, epididymis, and accessory glands are the external reproductive organs of the male goat. These structures are essential to the development, transportation, and storage of sperm.

PENIS: The penis is the male copulatory organ that facilitates the transfer of sperm during mating. It is made up of erectile tissue that swells with blood when excitement occurs, causing an erection and penetration during sexual activity.

SCROTUM: The testes are housed in the scrotum, a skin pouch that aids in controlling their temperature. Because the scrotum is external to the body cavity, the testes are able to maintain a temperature lower than the body, which is necessary for the creation of sperm.

TESTES: In male goats, the testes are the main reproductive organs that produce sperm and sex hormones like testosterone. Leydig cells, which generate testosterone, and seminiferous tubules, which create sperm, make up each testis.

EPIDIDYMIS: Sperm maturation and storage take place in the epididymis, a coiled tube that is found on the surface of each testis. The epididymis is where testicular sperm go through to acquire motility and the potential to fertilize.

ACCESSORY GLANDS: During ejaculation, the male goat's numerous accessory glands generate seminal fluid, which feeds and shields sperm. The prostate gland, bulbourethral glands, and seminal vesicles are examples of these glands.

INTERNAL ORGANS

The urethra, reproductive glands, and vas deferens are the internal organs of the male goat reproductive system. During ejaculation, these organs cooperate to move sperm from the testes to the surrounding area.

VAS DEFERENS: The main duct for sperm transportation, the vas deferens is a muscular tube that joins the urethra to the epididymis. Sperm pass through the vas deferens during ejaculation and exit the body through the urethra.

URETHRA: Urine and semen are transported from the bladder and reproductive glands, respectively, to the outside world through the urethra, a conduit. The urethra is the last route that sperm use during ejaculation, passing through the penis.

REPRODUCTIVE GLANDS: The production of seminal fluid is aided by the three primary reproductive glands found in male goats:

SEMINAL VESICLES: These structures secrete a fluid that is high in fructose and other nutrients, which feed sperm and give them energy to move.

PROSTATE GLAND: The fluid secreted by the prostate gland helps to balance the acidity of the vaginal tract and urethra, making the environment more favorable for sperm.

BULBOURETHRAL GLANDS: During ejaculation, the bulbourethral glands secrete a transparent, lubricating fluid that helps clean and lubricate the urethra.

Control of Hormones and Sperm Production

In male goats, the production of sperm is controlled by a complicated system of hormones generated by the pituitary, brain, testicles, and accessory glands. These hormones regulate both the generation of seminal fluid and the growth and maturation of sperm.

Gonadotropin-Releasing Hormone (GnRH): The pituitary gland releases luteinizing hormone (LH) and follicle-stimulating hormone (FSH) in response to the production of GnRH by the hypothalamus.

Luteinizing Hormone (LH): LH causes the testes' Leydig cells to produce more testosterone. The development of secondary sexual traits and sperm production, or spermatogenesis, depend on testosterone.

Follicle-Stimulating Hormone (FSH): The hormone called follicle-stimulating hormone (FSH) causes the seminiferous tubules in the testes to proliferate and release sperm. Additionally, it controls the maturation of sperm and testicular function.

Testosterone: The main hormone involved in male sex, testosterone, is necessary for spermatogenesis, desire, and secondary sexual traits including muscular growth and voice deepening.

Spermatogenesis

The process by which sperm cells are created and develop in the testes' seminiferous tubules is known as spermatogenesis. There are multiple steps in this intricate process, including:

- ✓ **SPERMATOGONIA:** Found in the walls of the seminiferous tubules, spermatogonia are the precursor cells for the generation of sperm. In order to create main spermatocytes, they go through mitosis.
- ✓ **PRIMARY SPERMATOCYTES:** To create secondary spermatocytes, primary spermatocytes go through meiosis I.
- ✓ **SECONDARY SPERMATOCYTES:** To create haploid spermatids, secondary spermatocytes go through meiosis II.
- ✓ **SPERMATIDS:** Spermatids mature and develop further to become sperm cells, or spermatozoa.

Sperm cells pass via the epididymis to mature and store after being released into the lumen of the seminiferous tubules. During mating, mature sperm cells can move and fertilize an egg.

The Production of Seminal Fluid and Ejaculation

The male goat's reproductive system expels seminal fluid and sperm through the urethra and penis during ejaculation. Ejaculation is a multi-step, intricate process that includes:

- ✓ **Arousal:** Arousal during sexual activity causes the release of neurotransmitters that increase blood flow to the penis' erectile tissue and cause an erection.
- ✓ **Production of Seminal Fluid:** Sperm from the epididymis combines with seminal fluid produced by the accessory glands, such as the seminal vesicles, prostate gland, and bulbourethral glands, to make semen.
- ✓ **Ejaculation:** Semen is propelled down the urethra and out of the penis by rhythmic contractions of the muscles in the vas deferens and accessory glands.

Factors Influencing the Health of Male Reproduction

Goats' male reproductive health is influenced by a variety of factors, including environmental factors and genetic predispositions. Farmers and breeders can maximize male fertility and reproductive success in their herds by being aware of these elements. Goats' male reproductive health is influenced by the following important factors:

- ✓ **Genetic Factors:** Male reproductive health is significantly influenced by genetics. Reproductive success, sperm quality, and fertility can all be impacted by certain genetic features. A herd's reproductive health can be preserved and even improved by breeding from males who are healthy, fertile, and possess desirable qualities.
- ✓ **AGE:** Men's reproductive health can be impacted by age. Older males may have a drop in fertility, whereas younger bucks may have lower sperm counts and less established reproductive systems. Age-related problems can be lessened with the right breeding and management techniques.
- ✓ **NUTRITION:** Sustaining the health of a man's reproductive system requires enough nutrition. Deficits in nutrition can result in fewer and lower-quality sperm. Providing a well-balanced diet full of vital vitamins, minerals, and nutrients helps encourage healthy reproduction.
- ✓ **BODY CONDITION:** A male goat's physical state can have an impact on his ability to reproduce. Goats that are underweight or overweight may have reproductive problems. Reproductive success depends on maintaining a healthy bodily state through appropriate nutrition and management techniques.

- ✓ **ENVIRONMENTAL ELEMENTS:** Stress, humidity, and temperature are a few examples of environmental elements that might affect the health of male reproduction. For instance, heat stress might lower the quantity and quality of sperm. Keeping goats in a relaxed and pleasant atmosphere can support the preservation of their reproductive health.
- ✓ **DISEASE AND PARASITES:** The reproductive health of men can be impacted by diseases and parasites. Reproductive abnormalities can be caused by certain diseases, such as caprine arthritis encephalitis (CAE) and brucellosis. These problems can be avoided with regular vaccinations, parasite management, and health monitoring.
- ✓ **MANAGEMENT TECHNIQUES:** Breeding plans, handling, and housing are examples of management techniques that can affect the reproductive health of males. Reproductive success can be increased and stress can be decreased by providing appropriate handling and shelter. Furthermore, enhancing genetic variety and fertility can be achieved through the implementation of efficient breeding programs.
- ✓ **TOXICITY:** Male reproductive health may be impacted by exposure to toxic substances such as pesticides, heavy metals, and certain plants. Reproductive problems can be avoided by keeping

goats protected from these chemicals and by creating a safe environment for them.
- ✓ **TRAUMA AND INJURIES:** Trauma or injuries to the reproductive system might affect a man's ability to conceive. Reproductive health can be enhanced and injuries can be avoided with proper handling and care.
- ✓ **BREEDING SOUNDNESS EXAMINATION (BSE):** Regularly doing BSEs might aid in evaluating the health of male reproductive systems. In order to determine whether bucks are suitable for mating, a BSE usually involves assessing physical and reproductive characteristics, such as semen quality, libido, and reproductive tract health.
- ✓ **TEMPERATURE:** The generation and viability of sperm depend on the proper regulation of temperature. Spermatogenesis requires the testes to remain at a slightly lower temperature than the rest of the body, which is maintained by the scrotum.

Breeders and farmers may help maintain and improve male reproductive health in their goat herds, guaranteeing optimal fertility and reproductive success, by addressing these issues and putting suitable management techniques in place.

The Impact of Hormones on Reproduction

The regulation of reproductive processes in both male and female goats is greatly influenced by hormones. These chemical messengers regulate reproductive processes by acting on target tissues and are produced by different organs and glands in the body. Comprehending the impact of hormones on reproduction is crucial for overseeing breeding initiatives and guaranteeing successful reproduction within goat populations. Here's a thorough examination of the ways that hormones affect goat reproduction:

1. **Gonadotropin-Releasing Hormone (GnRH):** Follicle-stimulating hormone (FSH) and luteinizing hormone (LH), two significant hormones released by the pituitary gland, are stimulated by gonadotropin-releasing hormone (GnRH), which is produced by the hypothalamus. For both male and female goats to begin their reproductive cycles, GnRH is necessary.

2. **Follicle-Stimulating Hormone (FSH):** The pituitary gland secretes FSH, which is essential for the growth of ovarian follicles in female goats. FSH causes the testes to produce more sperm in males. Females' FSH levels vary during the estrous cycle, reaching their maximum right before ovulation.

3. Luteinizing Hormone (LH): The pituitary gland also releases LH, which is responsible for a number of vital processes in both male and female goats. LH causes ovulation in females and promotes the development of the corpus luteum, which generates progesterone. LH in males causes the testicular Leydig cells to produce more testosterone.

4. Estrogen: In female goats, the ovaries are the main source of this group of hormones. In addition to facilitating the development of secondary sexual traits and priming the reproductive system for mating and fertilization, estrogen is essential for controlling the estrous cycle. The hour before ovulation is when estrogen levels rise.

5. Progesterone: After ovulation, the corpus luteum in female goats produces progesterone. Because it promotes early embryonic development and gets the uterine lining ready for implantation, progesterone is essential for sustaining pregnancy. Progesterone levels fall in the absence of pregnancy, which causes the corpus luteum to recede and a new estrous cycle to begin.

6. Testosterone: In male goats, the testes produce the main male sex hormone, testosterone. The development of male reproductive organs, secondary sexual traits, and sperm production all depend on testosterone. Seasonal variations in day length cause testosterone levels to fluctuate, peaking during the breeding season.

7. Prolactin: In female goats, the pituitary gland secretes this hormone, which is involved in breastfeeding and maternal behavior. During pregnancy and lactation, prolactin levels rise to promote the production of milk.

8. Oxytocin: The pituitary gland secretes the hormone oxytocin, which is involved in both the ejection of milk during feeding and the contraction of uteruses during labor. Goats require oxytocin during lactation and parturition.

9. Inhibin: The hormone known as inhibitin is secreted by the testes and ovaries and it prevents the pituitary gland from releasing growth hormone (FSH). Inhibin helps control the menstrual cycle in females by preventing FSH from being produced, and it helps control the creation of sperm in males by preventing FSH from being released.

10. Relaxin: The hormone relaxin, which the placenta and ovaries produce, aids in preparing the reproductive system for pregnancy and childbirth. Relaxin facilitates the fetus's easier passage during parturition by relaxing the ligaments and muscles in the pelvic area.

These hormones cooperate in a well-balanced system to control goat reproductive functions. Breeders and farmers may better manage breeding programs, maximize reproductive performance, and guarantee the health and welfare of their goat herds by having a better understanding of the role hormones play in reproduction.

GOAT MATING GUIDE   John William Bush (The Farmer's House)

Chapter 3: The Indication of Heat

How to Spot Heat Signs in Female Goats

A key component of successful goat breeding is heat detection, which enables breeders to choose the ideal moment for artificial insemination or mating. Breeders need to be aware of the estrus cycle and how to spot the telltale indications of heat in female goats. The estrus cycle, heat symptoms in female goats, and useful advice for spotting heat will all be covered in this chapter.

Successful heat detection and breeding of female goats depend on being able to identify the indicators of heat in them. Goats may exhibit several symptoms while they are in heat, however some typical ones include:

INCREASED VOCALIZATION: When a buck approaches a female goat in heat, she may vocalize more frequently.

RESTLESSNESS: During the heat, goats may pace or meander around the enclosure.

TAIL WAVING: When a female goat is in heat, she may wag her tail more frequently, especially if a buck is nearby.

MUCOUS DISCHARGE: A prominent indicator of heat in female goats is a clear, stringy mucous discharge from the vulva.

SWOLLEN VULVA: A goat in heat may have a larger, more noticeable vulva than usual.

MOUNTING BEHAVIOR: Although mounting behavior is more frequently linked to male goats, female goats who are in heat can also display mounting behavior, particularly when they are interacting with other female goats.

CHANGES IN APPETITE: When a female goat is in heat, she may go through phases of change in her appetite or eating patterns.

SEEKING OUT BUCKS: Goat females in heat have been seen to actively seek out and exhibit responsive behavior toward bucks.

ADVICE ON HOW TO DETECT HEAT

1. Observation: Take the time to watch your goats every day so you can get to know their habits and see any changes that might be signs of heat.

2. Maintaining Records: To aid in the prediction of subsequent cycles, keep thorough records on heat cycles, breeding dates, and any observations pertaining to heat behavior.

3. Use of Bucks: Add a buck to the herd and watch how the does behave. When the buck approaches a doe that remains still, she is probably in heat and ready to reproduce.

4. Heat Detection Aids: To determine whether a doe has been mounted by a buck, some breeders utilize heat detection aids, such as crayons or marked harnesses.

5. Professional Help: Consult a veterinarian or seasoned breeder for guidance if you have any questions about heat detection or breeding.

Successful breeding requires an understanding of the estrus cycle and the ability to spot the symptoms of heat in female goats. You can raise the likelihood of a successful mating by paying attention to your goats' behavior and employing suitable heat detecting techniques to increase heat detection accuracy.

Comprehending the Estrus Cycle

For goat breeding to be effective, it is essential to comprehend the estrus cycle. The recurrent physiological changes that take place in the female goat reproductive system are called the estrus cycle, sometimes referred to as the reproductive cycle or the heat cycle. Four phases make up this cycle, which is controlled by a complicated interaction of hormones: proestrus, estrus, metestrus, and diestrus. Let's examine each phase in more depth:

1. PROESTRUS: Proestrus, which lasts for one to three days, is the first phase of the estrus cycle. The ovaries start to generate follicles at this stage, which are sacs filled with fluid that contain immature eggs (oocytes). An increase in estrogen primes the reproductive system for fertilization. The doe may show signs of increased tail wagging, frequent urine, and restlessness. She is not yet open to mating, though.

2. ESTRUS: The phase of sexual receptivity that follows ovulation is known as "heat," or estrus. Although it might vary from goat to goat, estrus usually lasts one to three days. When estrogen levels reach their peak, the pituitary gland releases luteinizing hormone (LH), which promotes ovulation. During estrus, the doe is open to mating and may show mounting behavior if a buck approaches her. Increased vocalization, restlessness, and mucus discharge from the vulva are additional indicators of estrus.

3. METESTRUS: Following ovulation, the menstrual cycle is a period of transition. The broken follicle creates the corpus luteum, a tissue that secretes progesterone, during metestrus. The uterus becomes ready for pregnancy when progesterone levels start to rise. During metestrus, the doe is no longer open to mating.

4. DIESTRUS: The longest phase of the estrus cycle, diestrus is marked by elevated progesterone levels. The corpus luteum continues to produce progesterone to sustain pregnancy if fertilization does place. The corpus luteum regresses, progesterone levels drop, and a new estrus cycle starts if fertilization is unsuccessful.

ELEMENTS INFLUENCING THE ESTRUS CYCLE

Goats' estrus cycle can be influenced by a number of circumstances, such as:

NUTRITION: Sustaining regular estrus cycles requires a sufficient diet. Uneven or nonexistent cycles may result from nutritional deficits.

PHOTOPERIOD: Goats' estrus cycles can be influenced by the duration of the day. Estrus cycles can begin in the fall and winter as the days are shorter, while ovulation can be triggered by longer days in the spring and summer.

TEMPERATURE: Goats' estrus cycles can be impacted by severe weather, both in terms of timing and length. Specifically, heat stress can interfere with regular cycle rhythms.

HEALTH STATUS: A goat's general state of health can affect its estrus cycle. The occurrence and regularity of estrus cycles can be impacted by stress, illness, and reproductive abnormalities.

GENETICS: In goats, the duration and severity of estrus cycles can be influenced by genetic variables. Maintaining regular cycling patterns can be aided by breeding from animals that possess desired genetic features.

A thorough understanding of the estrus cycle is necessary for productive goat breeding. Breeders can enhance their breeding operations and raise their odds of successful reproduction by knowing the phases of the estrus cycle and the variables that can affect it.

FURTHER DETAILS REGARDING HEAT DETECTION TECHNIQUES

Breeders can determine when female goats are in estrus and prepared for mating by using heat detection, which is an essential component of successful goat breeding. Breeders can identify heat in goats using a variety of techniques, from ocular inspections to more sophisticated technical procedures. Breeders can increase breeding efficiency and reproductive success by being aware of these techniques and applying them skillfully. Here are a few typical techniques for detecting heat:

VISUAL OBSERVATION: One of the easiest and most economical ways to detect heat is through visual observation. Breeders can spot indicators of heat, such as restlessness, mounting behavior, and vocalization, by regularly observing their goats' behavior. A doe that is in heat may also have a vulva that is enlarged and discharges a transparent, stringy mucus.

TAIL PAINT OR CRAYONS: Marking the rump of a doe mounted by a buck can be accomplished with tail paint or crayons. Breeders can now quickly determine which does have been bred and follow their heat cycles thanks to this. The buck gets the paint or crayon on his chest or brisket, and it is transferred to the doe's rump when he mounts her.

AIDS FOR HEAT DETECTION: A variety of commercial heat detection tools are available, including chin-ball markers and marking harnesses. When the doe is mounted, these aids, which are fastened to the buck, leave a mark on her, signaling that she is in heat. Breeders with big herds or little time for observation may find these tools helpful.

HEAT DETECTION EQUIPMENT: To keep tabs on their goats' heat cycles, some breeders employ electronic heat detection equipment, such as activity monitors or electronic mount detectors. These tools can give more accurate information about when estrus occurs, and large-herd breeders may find them very helpful.

HORMONE TESTS: Goats' estrus cycle stage can be ascertained by hormone tests, such as progesterone tests. Breeders can determine the best time to breed by taking blood or milk samples, which can then be tested to assess hormone levels.

BEHAVIOR MONITORING: Behavioral alterations in goats may potentially be a sign of heat. A doe that is in heat, for instance, could become more talkative, agitated, and more interested in the buck. These behavioral indicators can be used by breeders to determine a doe's estrus.

ULTRASONOGRAPHY: This technique can be used to see goat reproductive organs and track the growth of follicles. Breeders can use this method to forecast ovulation and identify the estrus cycle stage.

Breeders can increase their accuracy in detecting heat in goats by combining different heat detection techniques. Breeders can improve the efficiency and success of their reproduction by paying close attention to the behavior of their goats, employing technological instruments, and deploying heat detecting devices.

Chapter 4: Strategies and Methods for Breeding

Natural or Organic Mating

Whether raising goats for meat, milk, or fiber, breeding is an essential part of the process. One of the most popular breeding techniques employed by goat farmers is natural mating. The natural mating process will be covered in this chapter, along with breeding methods, breeding stock selection, and best practices for effective natural mating.

BREEDING STOCK SELECTION

An effective natural mating process depends on choosing the appropriate breeding stock. Take into account the following elements while selecting goats for breeding:

HEALTH: Make sure that neither the female nor the male goats have any illnesses or genetic flaws that might affect their progeny.

CONFORMATION: Look for goats who have right breed features, robust, healthy bodies, and good conformation.

REPRODUCTIVE HISTORY: Take into account the reproductive histories of the goats, both male and female.

Select goats with a track record of successful matings and regular heat cycles.

PEDIGREE: Seek out goats possessing favorable genetic features and robust pedigrees. Enhancing the quality of the progeny can be achieved through breeding animals with established genetic makeup.

TEMPERAMENT: Select goats with amiable dispositions; aggressive or extremely shy goats may find it difficult to mate spontaneously.

BREEDING METHODS

permitting the male and female goats to mate naturally means not permitting any human interference. The following advice can help with natural mating success:

When the female goats come into heat, introduce them to the buck. When mounted, the doe will exhibit receptive behaviors such tail wagging, vocalization, and standing still.

OBSERVE MATING: Keep an eye on the mating process to make sure it goes well. The doe should be fully penetrated by the buck, which should mount her from behind.

GIVE THE GOATS TIME TO RELAX: Give the goats time to relax in between attempting to mate. Because mating can be physically taxing, it's critical to give the buck and the doe time to recover in between mating bouts.

ROTATE BUCKS: To avoid overuse and guarantee genetic diversity in the progeny, think about alternating your bucks if you have more than one.

OBSERVE BEHAVIOR: Keep an eye out for indicators of a successful mating attempt, such as the doe remaining still while mounted and showing less receptivity following the mating process.

OPTIMAL PROCEDURES FOR ORGANIC MATING

Take into account the following recommended steps to increase the likelihood of a successful natural mating:

- ➢ **Appropriate Nutrition:** To maintain reproductive health, make sure the male and female goats are getting enough food.
- ➢ **Health Care:** Make sure your goats are healthy on a regular basis and take quick action to address any infections or parasites.
- ➢ **Record Keeping:** To monitor your goats' reproductive success, keep precise records on the dates of breeding, the length of heat cycles, and the mating behavior.

> **Observation:** Take the time to watch your goats to see whether they are successfully mating and to spot any symptoms of heat.

Goat breeding can be accomplished naturally and successfully through natural mating. Breeders can increase the likelihood of successful natural mating and the production of healthy offspring by choosing the appropriate breeding stock, employing appropriate breeding techniques, and adhering to best practices.

Artificial Insemination

In goat farming, artificial insemination (AI) is a popular reproductive technique with many benefits, such as improved genetics, disease prevention, and higher breeding yield. This chapter will go into great detail about artificial insemination (AI) in goats, including the equipment required, advantages, difficulties, and best practices.

In artificial insemination, a female goat's reproductive canal is supplied with semen in the absence of spontaneous mating. Using specialist equipment, the semen is extracted from a chosen man, processed, and then inseminated into the female's uterus or cervix.

ADVANTAGES OF ARTIFICIAL FERTILIZATION

1. GENETIC IMPROVEMENT: Breeders can enhance the general quality of their goat herds by using the semen of genetically superior males thanks to artificial intelligence. This aids in the breeding process for desired qualities like disease resistance, meat quality, and milk output.

2. DISEASE CONTROL: Because there is no direct physical contact between the male and female goats during mating, artificial intelligence (AI) lowers the possibility of disease transmission between animals.

3. ENHANCED BREEDING EFFICIENCY: Artificial Intelligence enables breeders to maximize breeding efficiency by producing more offspring by enabling the insemination of many females with a single semen ejaculation.

4. FLEXIBILITY: AI gives breeders the freedom to utilize the semen of distant or unavailable guys, increasing genetic variety and the pool of available genes.

5. COST-EFFECTIVENESS: Although AI technology may have greater setup costs at first, the long-term advantages in terms of genetic enhancement and disease control frequently offset the cost.

THE METHOD OF ARTIFICIAL INSEMINATION

SEMEN COLLECTION: Using an artificial vagina or electro ejaculation procedure, semen is extracted from a chosen male goat, referred to as the donor buck. Next, the quality of the semen is assessed, taking into account the sperm concentration, motility, and morphology.

SEMEN PROCESSING: To enhance its volume and vitality, the semen is diluted with an extender and debris-free after collecting. Nutrients and antioxidants are included in the extender to keep sperm viable while they are being stored.

PROCEDURE FOR INSEMINATION: There are several ways to carry out the insemination process, such as intrauterine insemination (IUI) and cervical insemination. A catheter is inserted into the uterus through the cervix during cervical insemination, and the semen is then placed close to the uterine horns. With IUI, a specialized insemination gun is used to deposit the semen straight into the uterus.

TOOLS REQUIRED FOR ARTIFICIAL FERTILIZATION

Semen Collection Equipment: This comprises an electro ejaculation device or artificial vagina to extract semen from the donor buck.

Equipment for Processing Semen: Centrifuges, solutions for extending the gel, and receptacles for storing the gel, like straws or vials, are among the tools used in the process.

Insemination Equipment: Speculums for cervical insemination, insemination guns, and insemination catheters are examples of insemination equipment.

Storage of Sperm: To preserve sperm viability during storage, semen straws or vials are kept in liquid nitrogen tanks at extremely low temperatures.

OBSTACLES AND THINGS TO THINK ABOUT

Breeders should be aware of the following issues and obstacles even though artificial insemination has several advantages:

1. Skill and Training: To carry out artificial insemination successfully, one must possess the necessary training and experience. Before doing AI treatments on their own, breeders should receive training and practice under supervision.

2. *Timing:* Since AI must occur during the female goat's estrus cycle, timing is essential to its success. To maximize timing and raise conception rates, synchronization techniques and breeding protocols can be applied.

3. *Semen Quality:* Success rates for AI are greatly impacted by the quality of the semen used. For sperm to remain viable and motile, ideal conditions for sperm collection and processing must be met.

4. *Costs:* The initial outlay for semen processing and AI technology can be substantial. In comparing artificial intelligence (AI) to natural mating, breeders should take into account many parameters, including herd size, breeding objectives, and resource availability.

TOP TECHNIQUES FOR EFFECTIVE ARTIFICIAL INSEMINATION

1. *Estrus Synchronization:* During a certain breeding window, maximize time and enhance the number of females available for AI by implementing estrus synchronization protocols.

2. *Quality Control:* To guarantee high-quality semen for artificial intelligence, stringent quality control procedures should be put in place for the collection, processing, and storage of semen.

3. *Expert Staff:* To guarantee accuracy and reduce the possibility of problems, have expert staff members or veterinarians carry out AI procedures.

4. *Keeping Records:* To monitor success and make wise breeding decisions, keep thorough records of AI procedures, breeding dates, semen quality, and pregnancy results.

Goat breeders that want to enhance breeding efficiency, manage disease transmission, and improve genetics will find artificial insemination to be a useful tool. Breeders can apply AI successfully and accomplish their breeding objectives by comprehending the process, utilizing the right tools and methods, resolving issues, and adhering to best practices.

Selective Breeding and Line Breeding

Goat breeders employ two key methods to enhance desirable qualities in their herds: line breeding and selective breeding. With these methods, breeding stock is carefully chosen based on a number of factors, including productivity, conformation, and disease resistance. The ideas of selective breeding and line breeding will be covered in this chapter, along with their advantages, difficulties, and optimal application techniques.

SELECTIVE BREEDING

The deliberate breeding of animals with desired features to generate offspring with those same traits is called selective breeding, or artificial selection. Animals with characteristics like high milk production, quick development rates, or disease resistance are identified by breeders, who then carefully choose and breed these animals to pass on these features to the next generation.

THE ADVANTAGES OF SELECTED BREEDING

1. Genetic Improvement: Breeders can enhance particular characteristics within a population, including milk yield, meat quality, or fiber yield, by using selective breeding.

2. Adaptation to Environment: By breeding for features that improve an animal's chances of surviving and producing under particular circumstances, selective breeding can aid an animal's adaptation to its surroundings.

3. Disease Resistance: Breeders can lower the prevalence of diseases within a herd and enhance the general health of the herd by deliberately breeding for disease resistance.

4. Enhanced Uniformity: Selective breeding has the potential to enhance population uniformity, which facilitates the prediction of offspring traits.

DIFFICULTIES IN SELECTIVE BREEDING

1. Limited Genetic Diversity: The practice of selective breeding may result in a population's genetic diversity being reduced. This may raise the risk of genetic illnesses and make the population less able to adapt to changing environmental conditions.

2. Time and Resources: Careful planning, documentation, and stock monitoring are necessary for selective breeding, and these tasks can take a lot of time and resources.

3. Unintended Consequences: Breeding just for a desired trait may unintentionally result in the loss of other desirable traits or the selection of undesirable traits.

GUIDELINES FOR EFFICIENT SELECTIVE BREEDING

1. Establish Breeding Objectives: Clearly state the qualities you want your herd to retain or develop, then rank them in order of significance for your breeding plan.

2. Carefully Select Breeding Stock: Pick stock that possesses the required qualities and has a strong genetic foundation for those qualities.

3. Preserve Genetic Diversity: Occasionally add fresh genetic material from outside sources to your herd to help prevent the harmful effects of inbreeding.

4. Track and Assess Progress: To make sure you are moving closer to your breeding objectives, evaluate the performance of your breeding stock and their progeny regularly.

LINE BREEDING

Animals are bred within a particular family line to preserve or improve desired qualities. This is known as line breeding, a type of selective breeding. To "fix" particular qualities within a population and preserve genetic variability, line breeding is frequently employed.

THE ADVANTAGES OF LINE BREEDING

1. Genetic Fixation: A population's desired features can be fixed by line breeding, increasing its predictability in subsequent generations.

2. Preservation of Genetic Diversity: Line breeding permits some degree of outbreeding, which contributes to the preservation of genetic diversity, in contrast to inbreeding, which entails breeding closely related animals.

3. Selection for Particular Features: Using line breeding, breeders can concentrate on and selectively breed for particular qualities within a population, such as coat color or milk output.

THE DIFFICULTIES OF LINE BREEDING

1. Risk of Inbreeding: Line breeding entails some risk of genetic diseases and reduced fertility, but it is less likely than traditional inbreeding to result in inbreeding depression.

2. Limited Genetic Variation: A population's capacity to adapt to shifting environmental conditions may be hampered by line breeding, which can result in a loss of genetic variation within the population.

GUIDELINES FOR OPTIMAL LINE BREEDING

1. Maintain Records: To monitor the inheritance of traits and prevent unforeseen repercussions, keep thorough records of the lineage and performance of your breeding stock.

2. Track Genetic Diversity: To preserve genetic vigor, periodically evaluate the genetic diversity of your herd and think about adding new genetic material.

3. Steer Clear of Close Inbreeding: Although line breeding entails breeding within a particular family line, close inbreeding should be avoided in order to reduce the danger of genetic problems.

Goat breeders who want to enhance particular features in their herds might benefit greatly from the use of selective breeding and line-breeding. Breeders can increase the productivity, health, and adaptability of their goats by using these strategies to carefully select breeding stock, maintain genetic diversity, and track growth.

Chapter 5: Gestation and Pregnancy

Verifying the Pregnancy

A goat's pregnancy and gestation are essential life phases that result in the delivery of healthy progeny. The confirmation of pregnancy in goats, including pregnancy symptoms, pregnancy detection techniques, and optimal goat management techniques, will be the main topics of this chapter.

GOAT PREGNANCY SIGNS

Numerous indicators of pregnancy can be seen in goats, albeit they can differ based on the particular goat and stage of pregnancy. Among the typical indicators of a goat's pregnancy are:

1. MODIFICATIONS IN APPETITE: Goats going through pregnancy may exhibit variations in appetite, such as an increase or reduction in food intake.

2. ABDOMINAL ENLARGEMENT: As a pregnancy develops, a pregnant goat's abdomen will progressively grow as the fetus grows.

3. BEHAVIOR CHANGES: Pregnant goats may display a variety of behavioral changes, including restlessness and a need for isolation.

4. UDDER DEVELOPMENT: A pregnant goat's udder may swell and take on a fuller appearance in its later stages of pregnancy as it gets ready to produce milk.

5. CHANGES IN FETAL MOVEMENT: The fetus may become felt or visible from the outside of the goat's belly as the pregnancy progresses.

TECHNIQUES FOR VERIFYING PREGNANCY

Goats can be tested for pregnancy in several ways, such as:

Ultrasound: This non-invasive technique visualizes the fetus inside the uterus by using sound waves. It can be used to verify pregnancy and track fetal growth as early as 30 days following breeding.

Blood Testing: Progesterone and pregnancy-associated glycoproteins (PAGs), which rise in pregnant goats, are two pregnancy-specific hormones that can be found via blood testing.

Rectal Palpation: This technique feels for the presence of the uterus and fetus by carefully placing a gloved hand into the goat's rectum. After 60 days of gestation, this approach is at its most effective.

Abdominal Palpation: This technique entails feeling the goat's belly to see if the uterus and fetus are there. Although it is less precise than rectal palpation, early pregnancy can benefit from this technique.

THE BEST WAYS TO HANDLE EXPECTANT GOATS

Pregnant goats need to be managed with extra caution to protect the health and welfare of the developing fetus as well as the dam. The following are some guidelines for caring for pregnant goats:

- **Adequate Nutrition:** To promote the growth and development of the fetus, pregnant goats need a well-balanced diet full of nutrients. Protein and energy content in the diet should be substantial, and vitamins and minerals should be added as needed.
- **Sufficient Housing:** To keep them comfortable and shielded from the weather, pregnant goats need to have a sufficient amount of shelter.
- **Regular Monitoring:** Keep an eye out for any indications of disease or distress in pregnant goats and, if necessary, seek veterinary attention.

> **Vaccination and Parasite Control:** To safeguard themselves and their progeny against illnesses and parasites, pregnant goats should get regular deworming and immunizations.

Verifying a goat's pregnancy is a crucial part of running a productive breeding operation. Breeders may guarantee the health and welfare of their pregnant goats and their kids by being aware of the indicators of pregnancy, applying the right diagnostic techniques, and giving their goats the care they need.

Gestational Period and Handling

A goat's gestation is a critical stage in its life cycle, during which the fetus grows and develops inside the uterus. The health and welfare of the developing fetus as well as the dam depend on proper gestational care. The gestation period in goats will be covered in this chapter, along with its length, phases, dietary needs, and general pregnancy care procedures.

Goat Gestation Period

The time from mating to kidding is known as the gestation period in goats, and it normally lasts between 145 and 155 days, with an average of about 150 days. However, some variables, including breed, age, and environmental circumstances, might affect the gestation period. To prepare their goats for kidding and to give them the right care throughout pregnancy, goat breeders should be informed of the typical gestation duration.

Gestational Stages

Goats go through multiple stages of gestation, each of which is distinguished by unique fetus developments and dam body modifications. These phases consist of:

EARLY GESTATION (DAYS 1-45): The placenta starts to grow and the fertilized egg implants in the uterus during this phase of gestation. The main organs and structures start to form as the embryo divides and differentiates its cells quickly. The fetus is so little at this point that it might not be palpable or detectable using ultrasound technology.

MID GESTATION (DAYS 45–90): The fetus has grown considerably at this point and can be felt more readily via the pregnant goat's tummy. The placenta keeps expanding and developing while giving the fetus oxygen and nourishment. At this point, the fetus starts to take on the appearance of a tiny goat, and the mother may be able to feel its movements.

LATE GESTATION (DAYS 90-145+): The fetus grows and develops quickly during the last few days of pregnancy. When the fetus grows, the pregnant goat's abdomen enlarges visibly, and as it gets ready to nurse, the udder may start to swell and develop. In addition, the pregnant goat might display nesting behavior, such as looking for a private, peaceful place to give birth.

THE DIETARY NEEDS DURING PREGNANCY

To maintain the health of the pregnant goat and to promote the growth and development of the fetus, a proper diet is essential during gestation. Goats that are pregnant need a diet rich in protein, energy, vitamins, and minerals. Among the most important nutritional factors for pregnant goats are:

ENERGY: To maintain the growth and development of the fetus, pregnant goats need more energy. Grain should be added to high-quality fodder, like alfalfa or clover hay, to help them achieve their energy requirements.

PROTEIN: Both the health of the expectant goat and the growth and development of the fetus depend on protein. Goats that are expecting should be fed a diet strong in protein, which should include grains like oats or barley and legumes like soybeans or alfalfa.

VITAMINS AND MINERALS: To support fetal development and preserve the health of the dam, pregnant goats need higher doses of vitamins and minerals, especially vitamin A, vitamin E, calcium, and phosphorus. To meet their needs, a diet high in leafy greens, like spinach or kale, and mineral supplements should be given.

WATER: To promote fetal development and preserve hydration, pregnant goats need to have constant access to clean, fresh water. There should always be access to clean, uncontaminated water.

GENERAL HEALTHCARE PROCEDURES DURING PREGNANCY

Pregnant goats need extra care and attention to maintain their health and wellbeing in addition to eating a healthy diet. Among the standard procedures for taking care of pregnant goats are:

Frequent Monitoring: Keep an eye out for any symptoms of disease or suffering, such as alterations in behavior, appetite, or udder growth, in pregnant goats. If necessary, seek veterinarian care.

Appropriate Housing: To keep pregnant goats comfortable and shielded from the weather, give them a large enough shelter. Goats that are expecting should have access to a dry, clean place to rest without interruption.

Exercise: To preserve their general health and muscular tone, pregnant goats should be allowed to engage in frequent exercise. Goats that are pregnant shouldn't be overworked, especially if their gestation is late.

Vaccination and Parasite Control: To safeguard against illness and parasites, pregnant goats should have routine deworming and vaccines. Consult your veterinarian before giving any medication during pregnancy, as some vaccines and dewormers should be used carefully.

For pregnant goats and their young to be healthy and happy, proper care must be given during the gestation period. Goat breeders can contribute to the success of pregnancies and the birth of healthy children by knowing the gestation period, offering suitable feed, and adhering to general care procedures.

Typical Pregnancy Issues

Numerous variables, such as nutritional imbalances, environmental stressors, and infectious illnesses, can lead to pregnancy issues in goats. To reduce the likelihood of these issues and guarantee the health and well-being of the developing fetus as well as the dam, proper management and care are vital. This section will examine a few typical pregnancy issues in goats, along with their origins, signs, and remedies.

1. KETOSIS IN PREGNANCY TOXEMIA

Ketosis, another name for pregnancy toxemia, is a metabolic disease that develops when the fetus's energy needs are greater than the mother's capacity to provide them. This may cause the blood to become more concentrated in ketone bodies, which can cause symptoms including fatigue, decreased appetite, and weight loss.

- ➤ **CAUSES:** Inadequate nutrition, especially a diet high in fiber and low in calories, is a common cause of pregnancy toxemia. Goats that are overweight or obese may also experience it because high-fat reserves might disrupt the metabolism of carbohydrates.
- ➤ **SYMPTOMS:** In severe cases, pregnant toxemia can cause neurological symptoms like head pressure and aimless wandering in addition to fatigue, poor appetite, and weight loss.
- ➤ **PREVENTION:** Make sure pregnant goats are fed a balanced diet that satisfies their energy requirements to prevent pregnancy toxemia. To avoid obesity or unnecessarily losing weight, periodically assess your body's state and make necessary dietary adjustments.

> **TREATMENT:** Supplemental energy, such as propylene glycol or dextrose, is given to the affected goat to treat pregnant toxemia. Intravenous fluids may be required in extreme circumstances to treat electrolyte imbalances and dehydration.

2. TERMINATION/ABORTION

Any stage of pregnancy can result in abortion, which is the early ejection of the fetus. Several reasons, such as nutritional inadequacies, viral illnesses, and environmental stresses, can cause abortion.

> **CAUSES:** Infectious agents like Chlamydia, Toxoplasma, and Campylobacter can result in abortions in goats. Abortion can also result from nutritional deficits, such as a selenium shortage. Stressful environments, including intense heat or cold, can also cause abortions in goats that are pregnant.
> **SYMPTOMS:** Abortion symptoms might vary based on the underlying cause, however, they may include the evacuation of fetal tissues, uterine contractions, and vaginal discharge.
> **PREVENTION:** Keeping a clean, sanitary environment, offering a nutritious, well-balanced feed, and immunizing against infectious diseases

that can induce abortion are all important ways to prevent abortion in goats.

- ➤ **TREATMENT:** The course of action for a goat abortion is determined by the underlying cause. It may be necessary to prescribe antibiotics to treat infected abortion situations. Supplements can be used to make up for nutritional deficits, and environmental stressors should be kept to a minimum.

3. RETAINED FETAL MEMBRANE

When the placenta does not emerge from the uterus within 24 hours of giving birth, the condition known as retained fetal membranes or retained placenta occurs. If left untreated, this might result in infection and other problems.

- ➤ **CAUSES:** Inadequate uterine contractions, which can be brought on by stress, malnutrition, or hormonal imbalances, can result in retained fetal membranes.
- ➤ **SYMPTOMS:** Failed placenta expulsion within 24 hours of kidding, foul-smelling discharge, and infection symptoms including fever and lethargy are all possible indicators of retained fetal membranes.

- **PREVENTION:** Make sure pregnant goats are well-nourished and well-managed during their gestation period to avoid retained fetal membranes. When you see any symptoms of stress or disease, take quick action to address them.
- **TREATMENT:** If the placenta has not been evacuated within 24 hours, the placenta must be physically removed as part of the treatment for retained fetal membranes. Infections can be treated or prevented with antibiotics, and supportive care such as electrolytes and fluids may be required.

4. TWINNING

Goats frequently give birth to twins, a phenomenon known as twinning, which can provide difficulties for both the mother and the offspring. Pregnancy toxemia and dystocia, or painful delivery, are linked to twin pregnancies.

- **CAUSES:** Goat twinning is frequently brought about by hereditary factors, with some breeds having a higher propensity for twinning than others. The possibility of twinning can also be influenced by environmental factors, such as management techniques and diet.
- **SYMPTOMS:** An expanded abdomen, an increase in appetite, and behavioral changes like restlessness

or nesting behavior are all possible signs of twinning.
- ➢ **PREVENTION:** Although it is not possible to prevent twin pregnancies, there are management strategies that can help lower the risk of complications related to twinning, such as eating a balanced diet and keeping an eye out for symptoms of pregnancy toxemia.
- ➢ **TREATMENT:** To ensure that both kids are delivered safely, the dam must be closely observed during pregnancy and kidding in goats that are twinning. Assistance may be needed in cases of dystocia in order to birth the children safely.

5. ARTHRITIS/ METRITIS

An infection of the uterus known as metritis can develop following childbirth or an abortion. It is frequently brought on by bacteria that enter the uterus through the birth canal and can produce fever, foul-smelling discharge, and lethargic behavior, among other symptoms.

- ➢ **CAUSES:** Retained fetal membranes, traumatic births, and inadequate cleanliness during kidding are the most common causes of metritis in goats.
- ➢ **SYMPTOMS:** Fever, foul-smelling discharge, stomach pain, and indicators of disease like fatigue and appetite loss can all be indicators of metritis.

- ➢ **PREVENTION:** Keep the kidding area clean and sanitary, and keep a vigilant eye out for any signs of infection in the doe after kidding to prevent metritis.
- ➢ **TREATMENT:** Antibiotics are used to control the infection during metritis treatment, along with supportive measures like electrolytes and fluids. In severe situations, flushing the uterus may be necessary to get rid of the contaminated material.

Goats with pregnancy issues may experience major effects on both the developing fetus and the dam. To reduce the likelihood of these problems and guarantee the health and well-being of pregnant goats and their young, proper management and care are crucial during pregnancy. Breeders may safeguard their goats and guarantee good pregnancies by being aware of the origins, symptoms, prevention, and treatment of common pregnancy issues in goats.

Chapter 6: Birth and Kidding

Labor Signs in Female Goats

All kidding aside, the birthing process is an important part of a goat breeder's life. For the health of the dam and the newborn children, as well as to ensure healthy kidding, it is imperative to recognize the signals of labor. The indications of labor in goats, including the phases of labor, typical behaviors displayed by approaching parturition, and strategies for successful kidding, will all be covered in this chapter.

Signs of Labor in Goats

1. Behavior Changes: A pregnant doe may show signs of behavioral changes as labor draws near. She can start to get angrier and more restless, pacing or scratching the ground. While some DOES might become more talkative or affectionate, others might look for a peaceful, isolated spot to give birth.

2. Vulvar Swelling and Discharge: The doe's vulva may swell and relax in the days preceding kidding. A mucous plug, which can resemble a thick, jelly-like substance, or a clear, stringy discharge from the vulva may also be passed by her. These indicate that the doe's body is getting ready to give birth.

3. *Udder Development:* The first milk the doe produces, colostrum, is nutrient-rich and causes the udder to enlarge and fill. The teats may grow and become more noticeable, and the udder may feel constricted and glossy.

4. *Appetite Changes:* As parturition approaches, some DOES may notice a decrease in their appetite. This is typical and is thought to be caused by the expanding offspring pressing against the doe's stomach.

5. *Nesting Behavior:* Some DOES may display nesting behavior in the final days leading up to kidding. They might burrow in the bedding, paw at the ground, or make a nest-like space for giving birth. This is an instinctive action that aids the doe in creating a cozy and safe environment for her young.

6. *Pacing and Restlessness:* A doe may get more agitated as labor draws near. She could pace up and down, unable to settle in. This activity indicates that the doe is getting ready to give birth and that labor is about to begin.

7. *Lying Down and Rising:* The doe may frequently lie down and rise as labor goes on. This aids in positioning the babies for delivery and is a normal aspect of labor.

During contractions, the doe may also arch her back or extend her hind legs.

8. *Vocalization:* During labor, certainly DOES may make noises that range from gentle groans to louder bleats or cries. It is thought that by vocalizing, the doe not only draws attention from the goat breeder or the herd but also helps her deal with the discomfort of labor.

Labor Stages in Goats
Goat labor is usually split into three phases:

- **STATE ONE:** The doe may show indications of vulvar discharge, nesting behavior, and restlessness during this period. The uterus gets ready for contractions when the cervix starts to dilate. This phase may vary in duration according to the particular doe, ranging from several hours to a day or longer.
- **STAGE TWO:** The kids are born during this active period of labor. Each youngster will be delivered one at a time, with the doe going through intense, regular contractions. Though it might vary, the time between children is often less than an hour. During this phase, it's critical to keep a close eye on the doe and be ready to help if needed.
- **STAGE THREE:** The doe will pass the placenta, or afterbirth, once every child has been born.

Because a retained placenta can result in infection, this period is critical. After kidding, the placenta should pass within a few hours, and the doe needs to be cautiously watched for any indications of infection or retained placenta.

GETTING READY FOR KIDDING

It's crucial to have the following materials available in case of a kidding:

- Dry and spotless bedding for the kidding place
- Spotless cloths or towels to dry the children
- A sharp knife or sterile scissors to cut the umbilical cord
- Dipping the umbilical cord in iodine or another disinfectant
- Goat colostrum or colostrum replacement for nursing infants

Furthermore, confirm that the kidding area has access to fresh water, a source of heat if necessary, and is dry, warm, and clean. Keep a close eye out for any indications of labor in the pregnant doe, and be ready to offer assistance if needed.

It's critical to recognize the symptoms of labor in goats to ensure a healthy kidding experience and the well-being of the dam and her young. Goat breeders may assist in guaranteeing a smooth kidding process and the health and well-being of both the dam and the kids by being knowledgeable about the stages of labor, typical characteristics displayed by DOES approaching parturition, and how to prepare for kidding.

Helping with Challenging Births

A vital skill for goat breeders is helping with dystocia or difficult births. Several factors, such as the child's size or position, uterine inertia, or anatomical anomalies, can cause dystocia. Both the dam and the child may be saved if dystocia symptoms are identified and safe intervention techniques are used. Here offers a piece of comprehensive advice on helping with challenging goat births, covering how to spot dystocia symptoms, what to do to facilitate delivery, and when to call for veterinary help.

DYSTOCIA SYMPTOMS

1. Extended Labor: One of the most typical indications of dystocia is labor that continues over the usual time frame without any improvement in the kidding process. A doe may have dystocia if she has been in labor for several hours without showing any signs of giving birth.

2. Straining Without Progress: When a doe shows severe straining or pushing but shows no symptoms of giving birth, this is another indication of dystocia. This may suggest that the child is stuck or positioned strangely.

3. Abnormal Presentation: If a child is delivered in an unusual position, like sideways, head back, or breech (back end first), dystocia may result. The child's natural birth may be hampered or impossible by certain atypical appearances.

4. Absence of Fetal Membranes: Dystocia may be indicated if the doe has been in labor for some time and there are no indications that the fetal membranes are being passed. Fetal membranes are a necessary component of the birthing process; hence their absence may indicate an issue.

HOW TO HELP WITH CHALLENGING BIRTHS

- *Examine the Situation:* When helping with a challenging birth, the first step is to evaluate the circumstances. Calmly approach the doe and watch how she acts. Assess her for indications of dystocia and determine whether she is distressed.
- *Wash Hands and Equipment:* Use warm water and soap to give yourself a thorough hand wash before

helping with the birth. Put on sterile, clean gloves if at all possible. Make sure all of the supplies you use, including towels and lubricant, are sterile and clean.

- *Give Appropriate Restraint:* To keep the doe from moving too much throughout the procedure, softly yet firmly restrain her. This will help ensure the safety of the doe and the child during the birth process.
- *Examine Kid's Position:* After the doe has been securely secured, carefully examine the kid's position by sticking a gloved, lubricated hand inside her vagina. Take note of the child's orientation and posture to see if it is in an unusual position.
- *Correct posture:* Try carefully to realign the child if they are presented in an unusual posture, like breech or sideways. Gently and steadily press the child into the proper delivery position.
- *Help with Delivery:* After the buck is in the proper position, help the buck by gently pushing on it when it goes into labor. To prevent harm to the child or the doe, apply continuous, soft pressure.
- *Track Progress:* Keep an eye on how the delivery is going. Seek veterinary treatment right once if the delivery is not proceeding or if there are any signs of distress.

- ➤ ***Care for the Doe and the Baby:*** After the baby is born, make sure it can breathe by cleaning its mouth and nose. As long as the doe and her young are kept warm and dry, let them develop a relationship.
- ➤ ***Keep an Eye Out for difficulties:*** Following delivery, keep a watchful eye out for any indications of difficulties, such as heavy bleeding, weakness, or infection.
- ➤ ***Seek Veterinary Assistance:*** Get help from a veterinarian right away if you are unable to treat the dystocia or if there are any indications that things may get worse. For the doe's and her child's health and well-being, a veterinarian can offer extra care and support.

Helping with challenging births is a crucial ability for breeders of goats. Goat breeders may contribute to ensuring the safe birth of babies and the well-being of their herd by identifying the symptoms of dystocia and understanding how to properly intervene. Always be composed and cautious when handling a crisis, and get veterinarian help if necessary. The majority of dystocia situations can be effectively treated with the right care and attention, resulting in happy, healthy children.

Taking Care of Newborn Children

A key component of goat breeding is providing for the health, development, and general well-being of the young animals. Early childhood care can have a big impact on a child's development and help them make a smooth transition to adulthood. A thorough overview of caring for newborns is given in this chapter, covering issues like giving them colostrum, cleaning the umbilical cord, providing warmth and shelter, providing nutrition and water, and keeping an eye on their overall health.

COLOSTRUM FEEDING: Colostrum, the nutrient-rich first milk produced by the doe, is essential for newborn kids' health and immunity. It contains antibodies that provide passive immunity to protect against diseases and infections. Here are important considerations for colostrum feeding:

- ❖ **TIMING:** Kids should receive colostrum within the first few hours of life, ideally within the first 1-2 hours after birth. Colostrum absorption decreases rapidly after the first 24 hours.
- ❖ **QUANTITY:** Kids should receive approximately 10% of their body weight in colostrum during the first 24 hours. Divide this amount into multiple feedings if necessary.

- ❖ **BOTTLE FEEDING:** If the kid is unable to nurse from the doe, bottle feeding colostrum is necessary. Use a clean, sterilized bottle and teat to feed the colostrum to the kid.
- ❖ **COLOSTRUM REPLACER:** In cases where natural colostrum is not available, colostrum replacer or goat-specific colostrum can be used to provide essential nutrients and immunity to newborn kids.

CARE OF THE UMBILICAL CORD: Taking good care of the umbilical cord guarantees the child's health and helps avoid infection. Observe these recommendations for umbilical cord care:

- ❖ **LEAVE IT INTACT:** Let the umbilical cord decompose naturally and dry out. Premature cutting or tugging on the cord can cause bleeding and infection, so avoid doing so.
- ❖ **MAINTAIN IT CLEAN:** Make sure the area surrounding the umbilical cord is dry and clean. Steer clear of excessive moisture and contact with urine or feces as these can heighten the risk of infection.
- ❖ **INFECTION WATCH:** Keep an eye out for symptoms of infection, such as redness, swelling, discharge, or an unpleasant smell, in the area

surrounding the umbilical cord. If you think you may have an infection, see a veterinarian.

COMFORT AND SAFETY: Because they are sensitive to temperature changes, newborns need a warm, safe environment for their best development and well-being. Take into consideration the following advice when giving a newborn child shelter and warmth:

- ❖ **DRAFT-FREE ENVIRONMENT:** Make sure the kid's shelter or kidding area is well-insulated and free of drafts. Use bedding to add warmth and comfort, such as clean hay or straw.
- ❖ **HEAT SOURCE:** If a newborn is born in a cold environment or during a cold period, provide them with a heat source, such as a heat pad or lamp, to keep them warm.
- ❖ **MONITOR TEMPERATURE:** Keep an eye on the outside temperature to make sure it stays between 70 and 80°F (21 and 27°C), which is the ideal range for newborns.

NUTRITION AND HYDRATION: Newborns need proper nutrition and hydration for healthy growth and development. Adhere to these dietary and hydration recommendations:

- ❖ **MILK FEEDING:** Goats should be fed milk from their dam or a milk substitute that has been specially made for them. Give milk to your child four to six times a day at regular intervals to ensure proper nutrition.
- ❖ **WEANING:** Start the weaning process gradually when the animal is between four and six weeks old. To facilitate the transition to solid food, introduce solid food alongside milk feeding, such as kid-specific pellets or hay.
- ❖ **HYDRATION:** As soon as children begin eating solid food, give them access to clean, fresh water. Make sure that the water is clean and readily available.

MONITORING OF GENERAL HEALTH:

Frequent health monitoring enables timely intervention and early detection of any problems or concerns. Keep an eye on the following aspects of the health of newborns:

- ❖ **WEIGHT GAIN:** To ensure appropriate growth and development, track weight gain regularly. Children should gain weight in the first few weeks of life in a steady manner.
- ❖ **ACTIVITY LEVEL:** Pay attention to the conduct and level of activity of infants. Kids in good health are alert, curious, and active. Investigating any

indications of weakness, lethargic behavior, or unusual behavior is advised.

- ❖ **URINE AND FECES**: To guarantee proper digestive function, keep an eye on urine and feces production. Blood or mucus should not be present in well-formed, healthy feces. Urine ought to be odorless and transparent.

Taking Care of Infants

1. Bonding: After birth, let the mother and child form a close bond. This process of bonding lays the groundwork for a solid mother-offspring relationship and is essential to the child's development.

2. Drying Off: To keep the child from getting cold, dry off with a fresh towel if the weather is chilly or damp. After birth, make sure the child is kept dry and warm.

3. Identification: To keep track of your children, it's a good idea to identify each child if you have more than one. Leg bands, ear tags, and other identifying techniques can be used for this.

4. Navel Care: To avoid infection, dip the child's navel in iodine. Continue doing this each day until the navel has fully healed and dried up.

Medical Attention for Infants

VACCINATIONS: To find out the right vaccination schedule for your children, speak with your veterinarian. Immunizations can aid in preventing common ailments in goats, such as clostridial infections and tetanus.

DEWORMING: To avoid parasite infestations, children should have regular dewormings. To find out the right deworming schedule and products to use, speak with your veterinarian.

HEALTH MONITORING: Keep a careful eye out for any indications of illness or disease in your children. Children who are sick frequently exhibit lethargy, poor appetite, diarrhea, and respiratory symptoms.

HOOF TRIMMING: To avoid overgrowth and hoof issues, check the children's hooves regularly and trim them as necessary.

Taking care of newborns is an incredibly fulfilling yet difficult job. You can contribute to your child's health and well-being and lay a solid foundation for their future development by giving them the care they need from birth. Never forget to speak with your veterinarian about any worries you may have regarding the wellbeing or upbringing of your children. Your kids will mature into adult goats that are healthy and content if given the right care and attention.

Chapter 7: Handling Reproductive Health

Preventing and Treating Reproductive Disorders

Keeping your goats' reproductive systems under check is crucial to a productive breeding program. Maintaining the health and fertility of your herd can be achieved in part by treating and preventing reproductive problems. This chapter will give you a thorough overview of managing your goats' reproductive health, including how to treat common reproductive illnesses, identify warning signs of reproductive issues, and avoid reproductive disorders.

Stopping Reproductive Issues

APPROPRIATE DIET: Keeping your goats' reproductive health requires feeding them a well-balanced diet high in protein, vitamins, and minerals. Make sure your goats have access to fresh, clean water as well as wholesome grain or forage. For does to be in good enough condition for breeding and to be able to support healthy pregnancies, proper nutrition is essential.

SUFFICIENT EXERCISE: Encouraging your goats to exercise on a daily basis will help them stay healthy overall and avoid obesity, which may be harmful to their reproductive systems. Goats that exercise can become more fit and have more productive reproductive cycles. Encouraging your herd to exercise or have access to pasture is crucial to their well-being.

FREQUENT VETERINARY EXAMINATIONS: Make an appointment for routine examinations with your veterinarian to keep an eye on your goats' reproductive health and to handle any possible problems early. In addition to doing medical examinations and evaluating body conditions, your veterinarian can offer guidance on breeding management. In order to identify and prevent reproductive diseases, routine checkups are helpful.

CONTROL OF PARASITES: Your goats' reproductive health may suffer as a result of parasites. Put in place a parasite control strategy to stop infestations. Your herd's health depends on regular deworming, pasture management, and keeping an eye out for indications of parasite infection.

SUITABLE BREEDING PROCEDURES: To avoid reproductive issues, use appropriate breeding techniques, such as making sure bucks and does are healthy and of breeding age. In order to lower the possibility of genetic problems, steer clear of breeding closely related goats. Good breeding practices can contribute to healthy offspring and fruitful pregnancies.

Identifying the Symptoms of Reproductive Issues

UNABLE TO CONCEIVE: Goats often have infertility, which can be brought on by a number of variables such as age, diet, and overall health. Infertility symptoms might include abnormal menstrual periods, infertility, or recurrent miscarriages. Developing a treatment plan and identifying the underlying cause of infertility might be facilitated by speaking with your veterinarian.

> ➢ **TREATMENT:** To ascertain the underlying reason of infertility, speak with your veterinarian. Hormone therapy, nutritional supplements, and other therapies may be part of the treatment. Depending on the particular requirements of your goats, your veterinarian can advise you on the best course of action.

TERMINATIONS: Any stage of pregnancy can result in an abortion, which can be brought on by environmental causes, dietary deficits, or pathogenic agents. Vaginal discharge, uterine contractions, and the evacuation of fetal material are all possible indicators of an abortion. If your herd experiences abortions, it's critical to identify the underlying reason and work with your veterinarian to establish the best course of action.

> **TREATMENT:** If your herd experiences abortions, it's critical to identify the root reason. Tests can be run by your veterinarian to determine the cause and suggest the best course of action. In addition to treating any underlying medical conditions, supportive care for abortion patients may involve the use of fluids and antibiotics.

PLACENTA RETAINED: Failure to release the placenta after giving birth, or retained placenta, can result in infection and other issues. Retained placenta symptoms can include the doe exhibiting symptoms of sickness and an unpleasant-smelling discharge. For treatment options, speak with your veterinarian if a doe after kidding keeps her placenta.

> **TREATMENT:** See your veterinarian if a doe that has just given birth keeps her placenta after kidding. In order to prevent infection, treatment may entail manually removing the placenta and giving antibiotics. Depending on the particulars of the retained placenta, your veterinarian can advise on the best course of action.

Keeping your goats' reproductive systems under check is crucial to a productive breeding program. You may contribute to maintaining the health and fertility of your herd by treating common reproductive illnesses, avoiding them, and identifying the warning indications of such issues. Don't forget to collaborate closely with your veterinarian to create a thorough plan for managing your goats' reproductive health.

Immunizations and Maintaining Health

Keeping your goats' reproductive systems under check is essential to a productive breeding program. Goat reproductive system problems can be significantly reduced by vaccination and good health maintenance. Here will offer a comprehensive guidance on how to maintain your goats' reproductive health through vaccination and general health care procedures. It will cover topics such as the significance of immunization, prevalent reproductive illnesses, vaccination schedules, and general health care advice.

THE VALUE OF IMMUNIZATION

As vaccinations aid in the prevention of infectious diseases that could harm the reproductive system, they are an essential part of managing goat health. Vaccination provides immunity against some diseases by inducing the production of antibodies by the goat's immune system against certain pathogens. You can lower your goats' risk of reproductive issues and enhance the general health of your herd by vaccination them.

Typical Reproductive Illnesses

Goats' reproductive systems are susceptible to a number of illnesses. Among the most prevalent illnesses affecting reproduction are:

1. *Brucellosis:* A bacterial infection known as brucellosis can result in infertility, abortion, and decreased milk supply in goats. It can spread to people and is very contagious. In regions where brucellosis is common, vaccination is advised and is currently accessible.

2. *Caprine Arthritis Encephalitis (CAE):* A viral illness that can affect goats and result in encephalitis, mastitis, and arthritis. It is transmitted by milk and colostrum that are contaminated. Since there is currently no vaccine against CAE, management strategies including testing and isolating affected goats are the main means of prevention.

3. *Campylobacteriosis:* Infertility, miscarriage, and stillbirths in goats can result from the bacterial infection campylobacteriosis. For herds where there has been a history of campylobacteriosis, vaccination is advised and is currently accessible.

4. *Toxoplasmosis:* This parasite illness can result in stillbirths and abortions in goats. It is transmitted by consuming tainted food or drink. Since there is no vaccine against toxoplasmosis, management strategies include limiting access to tainted feed and water sources are the main means of prevention.

SCHEDULES FOR VACCINATIONS

Goat vaccination schedules should be customized to your herd's unique requirements and depending on variables like the age and reproductive status of your goats, the frequency of diseases in your area, and your management style. To create a vaccination regimen that is suitable for your herd, speak with your veterinarian. Goat vaccinations on a generic schedule could consist of:

KIDS: Colostrum from immunized animals should be given to children in order to give them passive protection against illness. Additionally, at 4-6 weeks of age, infants can receive the CDT vaccine, which protects against tetanus and Clostridium perfringens. Up until 16 weeks of age, booster doses are administered every 3–4 weeks.

BREEDING DOES: Prior to breeding, breeding does ought to receive vaccinations against diseases like leptospirosis, campylobacteriosis, and brucellosis. Your veterinarian may advise that you have booster injections every year.

ALL GOATS: To preserve immunity against illnesses like CDT, all goats should have an annual booster vaccine. Several immunizations might be advised in light of your herd's particular requirements.

Tips for Maintaining General Health

Several general health maintenance guidelines can help keep your goats healthy and prevent reproductive diseases in addition to vaccinations:

1. Nutrition: To maintain your goats' general health and ability to reproduce, feed them a well-balanced diet high in protein, vitamins, and minerals.

2. Cleanliness: To lower the chance of illness transmission, keep your goat facilities tidy and well-maintained.

3. Monitoring: Keep a close eye out for any symptoms of sickness in your goats, such as altered eating, behavior, or reproductive health.

4. *Quarantine:* To stop the spread of contagious diseases, quarantine new goats before integrating them into your herd.

5. *Parasite Control:* Since parasites can harm reproductive health, put in place a program to prevent infestations.

A good breeding program depends on you taking care of your goats' reproductive health through vaccinations and health maintenance procedures. You may contribute to maintaining the health and fertility of your herd by vaccinating your goats against common reproductive diseases, according to a customized vaccination schedule, and practicing general health maintenance techniques. Don't forget to collaborate closely with your veterinarian to create a thorough health management plan tailored to your goats' individual requirements.

Consumption of Foods for Reproductive Health

For goats to be healthy reproductively, nutrition is essential. Your goats will be in the best possible shape for mating and pregnancy if you provide them a balanced diet full of vital nutrients. This chapter will include a thorough explanation of the role that nutrition plays in reproductive health, the nutritional needs of breeding goats, and practical advice on feeding and monitoring your herd's nutrition.

Nutrition's Significance for Reproductive Health

Goats need a healthy diet to maintain their reproductive systems. Deficits in nutrition can cause infertility, delayed puberty, and low rates of pregnancy, among other reproductive issues. Conversely, an ideal diet can boost conception rates, enhance fertility, and promote healthy pregnancies.

The Dietary Needs of Goat Breeding

Goats raised for breeding have different nutritional needs based on where they are in the reproductive process. Goats raised for breeding need a diet high in calories, protein, vitamins, and minerals to meet their increased metabolic needs throughout the breeding season. The following are some essential dietary needs for goat breeding:

Energy: To sustain their elevated metabolic rate during breeding and pregnancy, breeding goats need a diet high in energy. Good quality forages, cereals, and vitamins can supply energy.

Protein: Protein is necessary for the growth and development of muscles as well as for reproductive processes. Goats raised for breeding purposes should eat a diet high in protein, which can be obtained from foods such alfalfa hay, legume meal, and soybean meal.

Vitamins and Minerals: To maintain their general health and ability to reproduce, breeding goats need sufficient levels of vitamins and minerals. Make sure the mineral supplement your goats are using is made especially for them.

Water: Breeding goats need water to stay healthy and properly hydrated. Make sure your goats always have access to fresh, clean water.

Feeding and Nutrition Management for Healthy Reproduction

Take into account the following advice to make sure your goats get the nourishment they require for the best possible reproductive health:

Balanced food: Feed your goats a food that satisfies their needs for protein, energy, vitamins, and minerals. See a veterinarian or nutritionist to create a feeding plan that is customized to your goats' individual requirements.

Fodder Quality: As a vital source of nutrition and energy, make sure your goats have access to high-quality fodder.

Keep an eye on the quality of your feed and add grains or vitamins as needed.

Body Condition: Keep a close eye on your goats' physical state and modify their nutrition as necessary. On a scale of 1 to 5, strive for a body condition score of 3 to 3.5 for goats. Goats that are too thin or too obese may have reproductive issues.

Mineral Supplementation: Give your goats a supplement containing minerals that is made especially for them. Make sure the supplement has all the necessary minerals, including selenium, phosphorus, and calcium.

Water: Make sure your goats always have access to fresh, clean water. Reproductive health can be adversely affected by dehydration.

For goats to be healthy reproductively, nutrition is essential. Your goats can be kept in peak reproductive and pregnant condition by feeding them a balanced diet that satisfies their needs for energy, protein, vitamins, and minerals. To preserve your goats' reproductive health, periodically check on their physical condition and make any dietary adjustments. Create a food plan specifically for your goats' needs by collaborating closely with a veterinarian or nutritionist.

Chapter 8: Breeding for Specific Goals

Breeding to Produce Milk

Goat breeders frequently breed their animals to provide milk, either for their own use or for commercial dairy farms. Dairy goat breeding success depends on choosing breeding stock with the proper genetics for maximum milk production. A thorough guidance on breeding goats for milk production, including important factors to take into account, breeding techniques, and management techniques to maximize milk production in your herd, is provided in this chapter.

The Value of Breeding to Produce Milk

A dairy goat herd that is productive must be maintained through breeding for milk production. Genetic variables affect milk production, thus choosing breeding stock with the proper genetic makeup is essential to producing large amounts of milk. Your dairy goat operation's overall productivity and profitability can be raised by breeding for milk output.

KEY CONSIDERATIONS IN BREEDING FOR MILK PRODUCTION

1. Breed Selection: Choose breeds of dairy goats that are renowned for producing large amounts of milk; examples of these breeds include Saanen, Nubian, Alpine, and LaMancha goats. Choose breeds that will help you achieve your milk production objectives because different breeds have varying capability for producing milk.

2. Genetic Selection: Seek out breeding stock possessing robust genetics for milk production. To determine their genetic potential for milk production, take into account the dam and sire's milk production records as well as those of any other relatives.

3. Body Condition: In order to boost milk production, breeding does need to be in good physical condition. Make sure they are neither underweight nor overweight since this may impair their capacity to yield milk.

4. Nutrition: Feed breeding does a healthy, well-balanced diet high in protein, energy, and minerals. Supporting milk production, particularly during breastfeeding, requires proper nutrition.

5. Management Techniques: Use techniques including routine milking, good udder care, and hygienic conditions in the milking area to support milk production. Your herd's milk output can be maximized with the use of proper management techniques.

BREEDING TECHNIQUES TO PRODUCE MILK

1. LINE BREEDING: Breeding related animals together, such as father-daughter or mother-son pairings, in order to concentrate desired qualities in the progeny is known as line breeding. You can utilize line breeding to correct traits in your herd that are linked to milk output.

2. CROSSBREEDING: Breeding animals from many breeds together to combine the best qualities from each breed is known as crossbreeding. You can introduce new genotypes for milk production into your herd through crossbreeding.

3. SELECTION CRITERIA: Take into account aspects including body condition, overall health, udder conformation, and milk production records while choosing breeding stock for milk production. Choose animals in your herd that exhibit the qualities you wish to see improved.

4. ARTIFICIAL INSEMINATION (AI): AI allows you to blend high-yielding sire genetics into your herd. With AI, you can choose sires that have the appropriate qualities for milk production without having to maintain a profit on your farm.

MANAGEMENT TECHNIQUES FOR THE PRODUCTION OF MILK

1. Appropriate Nutrition: Feed your dairy goats a well-balanced food that satisfies their needs for protein, energy, vitamins, and minerals. Supporting milk production requires proper nutrition.

2. Frequent Milking: To encourage milk production, milk your goats on a regular basis. For dairy goats to continue producing milk, they must be milked at least twice a day.

3. Udder Care: Take proper care of your udders to avoid mastitis and other problems. Maintain the udder dry and clean, and keep an eye out for any infection symptoms.

4. Sanitation: To avoid contaminating the milk, keep the milking area tidy and hygienic. Make sure milk is handled and stored correctly, and clean the milking equipment on a regular basis.

5. Health Monitoring: Keep a close eye on your dairy goats' well-being and take quick action to resolve any problems. Goats in better health have a greater chance of yielding more milk.

Goat breeding for milk production necessitates meticulous management procedures and careful selection of breeding material. You may maximize milk production in your dairy goat herd by choosing breeding stock with the appropriate genetics, putting good breeding tactics into practice, and adhering to good management practices. Don't forget to collaborate closely with your dietitian and veterinarian to create a breeding and management strategy tailored to your herd's unique requirements.

Breeding for High-Quality Meat

One important facet of goat farming, especially for those who are focused on meat production, is breeding goats for quality meat. Producing meat of superior quality requires careful selection of breeding stock with the appropriate genetic makeup. We will provide you a thorough guide on breeding goats for high-quality meat, complete with important factors to take into account, breeding techniques, and management techniques to maximize the quality of the meat in your herd.

Breeding Is Important for High-Quality Meat

To produce soft, tasty, and healthy meat products, it is essential to breed for meat quality. Numerous factors, like as genetics, diet, and management techniques, affect the quality of meat. You can boost the overall quality and marketability of your meat products by breeding goats for their meat, which will increase sales and satisfy customers.

IMPORTANT POINTERS FOR MEAT QUALITY BREEDING

Selecting a Breed: Goat breeds such as Boer, Kiko, Spanish, and Myotonic (fainting) goats are well-known for their exceptional meat quality. Choose breeds that will help you achieve your goals for meat quality as different breeds have distinct qualities.

Genetic Selection: Seek out breeding stock possessing robust genetics for meat quality. To determine their genetic potential for meat quality, take into account the sire, dam, and any other relatives' development rate, muscling, and carcass shape.

Growth Rate: In order to swiftly attain market weight, breeding stock should grow quickly. A key predictor of high-quality meat is rapid growth and effective feed conversion, so choose your breeding stock accordingly.

Good carcass conformation: With well-developed muscle and no fat deposition, is ideal for breeding stock. A well-conformed carcass is necessary to provide meat cuts with a good grade.

Nutrition: Feed breeding stock a healthy, well-balanced diet high in protein, energy, and minerals. A healthy diet is necessary to promote muscular growth and development, both of which are important for the quality of meat.

BREEDING TECHNIQUES FOR HIGH-QUALITY MEAT

Utilizing line breeding: You can improve your herd's desirable meat-quality features. Concentrating these features in the progeny can be achieved through breeding related animals, such as father-daughter or mother-son matings.

Crossbreeding: You can utilize crossbreeding to add new genetics to your herd that will improve the quality of the meat. Combining good qualities from each breed will help you increase the quality of meat in your herd by breeding animals of different breeds.

Selection Criteria: Growth rate, muscling, carcass shape, and general health are all important considerations when choosing breeding stock for meat quality. Choose animals in your herd that exhibit the qualities you wish to see improved.

Artificial Insemination (AI): AI allows you to cross-pollinate your herd with DNA from premium meat sires.

With AI, you can choose sires who possess the desired qualities for meat quality without having to maintain a profit on your farm.

MANAGEMENT STRATEGIES FOR HIGH-QUALITY MEAT

Appropriate food: Feed your meat goats a well-balanced food that satisfies their needs for protein, energy, vitamins, and minerals. A healthy diet is necessary to promote muscular growth and development, both of which are important for the quality of meat.

Exercise: To encourage muscular growth and general health, let your meat goats engage in frequent exercise. Exercise increases muscular tone and decreases fat deposition, both of which improve the quality of meat.

Health Monitoring: Keep a close eye on your meat goats' well-being and take quick action to resolve any problems. Healthy goats have a higher chance of normal growth and development, which results in higher-quality meat.

Slaughter Procedures: Follow the right procedures while slaughtering animals to preserve the quality of the meat. To reduce stress and preserve the quality of the meat, use humane slaughter procedures and appropriate carcass handling techniques.

Goat rearing for high-quality meat demands meticulous management procedures and careful selection of breeding stock. You may maximize meat quality in your meat goat herd by choosing breeding stock with the appropriate genetics, putting good breeding tactics into practice, and adhering to good management practices. Don't forget to collaborate closely with your dietitian and veterinarian to create a breeding and management strategy tailored to your herd's unique requirements.

Breeding for Display or Exhibition

A satisfying side of goat farming is producing goats for show or exhibition, which gives breeders the chance to exhibit their animals and compete for awards and acclaim. In order to produce animals that fulfill breed standards and perform well in the show ring, breeding for the show needs careful selection of breeding stock and meticulous attention to detail in management methods. In order to maximize performance in the show ring, we will offer a comprehensive guide on breeding goats for show or exhibition that covers important factors, breeding tactics, and management techniques.

The Value of Breeding for Exhibition or Show

Breeding for show or exhibition is crucial for demonstrating the caliber of your herd and for advancing and maintaining breed standards. Breeding for show goats necessitates choosing animals that meet the conformation, structure, and general appearance standards that are used to judge them. Moreover, breeding for display can raise the market value and general quality of your herd.

IMPORTANCE OF BREEDING FOR SHOW OR EXHIBITION

Breed Standards: Learn about the requirements set forth by the breed association of your choice. Breed standards delineate the optimal features and properties for every breed, encompassing physical attributes such as conformation and color. Choose breeding stock that largely complies with these requirements.

Genetic Selection: To succeed in shows, seek out breeding stock with good genetics. To determine their chances of success in the show ring, take into account the dam's and sire's show records in addition to those of any other relatives.

Conformation: In accordance with breed standards, breeding stock should be correctly conformed. Seek for creatures with level top lines, robust pasterns and feet, straight legs, and well-developed muscles. In the show ring, proper conformation is crucial for success.

Temperament: Calm and submissive temperaments are ideal for handling and exhibiting breeding stock. Choose animals that are docile and cooperative.

Health and Condition: To compete successfully in the show ring, breeding stock needs to be in good health and condition. Make certain that the animals are healthy, well-groomed, and displayed.

BREEDING TECHNIQUES FOR EXHIBITION OR SHOW

Line Breeding: Resolving conformation-related desired features through line breeding can help your herd succeed. Father-daughter or mother-son matings, for example, can help concentrate these features in the progeny.

Crossbreeding: You can employ crossbreeding to provide fresh genetics to your herd that will increase show success. Combining good qualities from each breed might assist boost your herd's show potential through animal breeding.

Selection Criteria: Take into account traits including conformation, temperament, general appearance, and health when choosing breeding stock for display or exhibition. Choose animals in your herd that exhibit the qualities you wish to see improved.

Using artificial insemination (AI): You can provide your herd access to genetics from superior show sires. With AI, you may choose sires who have the show qualities you want without having to maintain a profit on your farm.

MANAGEMENT PRACTICES FOR SHOW OR EXHIBITION

Appropriate Nutrition: Feed your show goats a well-balanced food that satisfies their needs for protein, energy, vitamins, and minerals. For growth and muscle development to be supported, which are necessary for show success, proper diet is vital.

Exercise: To encourage muscular tone and general health, let your show goats engage in frequent exercise. Exercise increases an animal's general appearance and conformation, which increases its competitiveness in the show ring.

Grooming: Show goats require proper grooming. Frequent grooming keeps animals tidier, improves their appearance, and enables assessors to make accurate judgments about their conformation and condition.

Training: Teach your show goats how to be handled and displayed properly. This covers leading, halter training, and judge-posing. Through training, animals can improve their comfort and self-assurance in the show ring.

Health Monitoring: Keep a close eye on your show goats' well-being and take quick action to resolve any problems. Goats in good health have a higher chance of excelling in the show ring and are less likely to be rejected for medical reasons.

Goat breeding for show or exhibition demands meticulous management procedures and careful selection of breeding stock. You may maximize success in the show ring by choosing breeding stock with the appropriate genetics, putting good breeding plans into operation, and adhering to appropriate management procedures. Don't forget to collaborate closely with your dietitian and veterinarian to create a breeding and care strategy tailored to your show goats' requirements.

GOAT MATING GUIDE   John William Bush (The Farmer's House)

Chapter 9: Maintaining Records and Managing Breeding Programs

Importance of Record Keeping

Maintaining accurate records is crucial to running a productive goat breeding operation. Breeders can monitor the health and performance of their animals, make well-informed decisions about breeding, and raise the general standard of their herd by keeping thorough records. The significance of record keeping in goat breeding, the kinds of records that should be kept, and the best methods for managing breeding programs and record keeping will all be covered in this chapter.

Keeping accurate records is essential to a healthy and productive herd of goats. Among the main justifications for the significance of record keeping in goat breeding are:

PERFORMANCE TRACKING: Breeders can monitor individual animals' growth rates, milk output, and reproductive success by keeping track of their records. Breeders can use this information to identify animals that perform well and to make well-informed breeding decisions.

HEALTH MONITORING: By keeping track of vaccinations, dewormings, and other health-related procedures, breeders can monitor the health of their herd with the use of records. Breeders can use this information to quickly identify and solve health issues.

BREEDING DECISIONS: Breeders can monitor parentage, genetic information, and breeding dates by keeping records. Making educated breeding decisions and enhancing the herd's general genetic makeup require this information.

FINANCIAL MANAGEMENT: Breeders can monitor their costs, earnings, and profitability with the use of records. Making wise business decisions and overseeing the financial components of a breeding program require this information.

Kinds of Documents to Maintain

Goat breeders need to maintain a variety of records in order to efficiently manage their breeding program. Among the important record kinds to maintain are:

INDIVIDUAL ANIMAL RECORDS: These should contain details about each animal, including breed, date of birth, gender, identification number, and any distinctive markings. Records should also include other data, such as performance metrics, health history, and reproductive history.

BREEDING RECORDS: Breeding dates, mating pairs, and any reproductive technology (like artificial insemination) should all be included in these records. Documenting pregnancy tests, due dates, and kidding results is also crucial.

HEALTH RECORDS: These should contain information about past vaccinations, dates of deworming, medical conditions, diagnoses, and any drugs prescribed. Breeders can monitor herd health and spot potential problems by keeping thorough medical records.

PRODUCTION RECORDS: Information about milk production, such as daily milk yield, milk composition (including fat and protein content), and lactation duration, should be recorded in these records. Records for meat goats may include weights, growth rates, and carcass quality.

Best Practices for Maintaining Records and Managing Breeding Programs

Breeders should adhere to these recommended practices in order to guarantee efficient record keeping and management of breeding programs:

- ➤ **EMPLOY A SYSTEM FOR RECORD-KEEPING:** To maintain track of your records, use a system designed specifically for that purpose, such as a spreadsheet or specialist software. Make sure the system has all the features your breeding program requires and is simple to use.
- ➤ **BE CONSISTENT:** Accurately and consistently record information. Standardize vocabulary and formats to make sure your documents are easy to read and comprehend.
- ➤ **MAINTAIN CURRENT RECORDS:** Ensure that all of your records reflect the most recent information. As new information becomes available, this includes updating breeding, health, and productivity data.
- ➤ **BACK UP YOUR RECORDS:** To guarantee that your records are shielded against destruction or loss, make regular backups of them. For backups, think about utilizing external hard drives or online storage.
- ➤ **EXAMINE AND ANALYZE YOUR RECORDS:** To spot trends and patterns, go through and examine your records on a regular basis. Make wise breeding decisions and enhance the administration of your breeding program as a whole by using this information.

Maintaining accurate records is crucial to running a productive goat breeding operation. Breeders may monitor the health and performance of their animals, make educated decisions about breeding, and raise the standard of their herd as a whole by maintaining thorough and accurate records. In order to keep their goat herd healthy and productive, breeders can benefit from adhering to best practices for record-keeping and breeding program management.

Establishing a Breeding Timetable

One of the most important aspects of running a productive goat breeding operation is developing a breeding timetable. A breeding calendar, which takes into account the reproductive cycle of the goat, the breeding season, and management objectives, helps ensure that breeding takes place at the best time for successful conception and kidding. Now let's talk about how to plan your goat herd's breeding calendar, covering important factors, techniques, and recommended procedures.

Key Considerations for Creating a Breeding Schedule

➢ **REPRODUCTIVE CYCLE:** Establishing a breeding program for goats requires an understanding of their reproductive cycle. Usually, the estrous cycle in female goats (does) lasts 21 days, during which the heat (estrus) lasts for 12 to 36 hours. For a good conception, breeding should take place during estrus.

➢ **BREEDING SEASON:** The length of the day and the surrounding conditions can have an impact on the breeding season of a lot of goat breeds. It is possible to guarantee that kidding takes place during ideal weather and that offspring have the best chance of surviving by breeding during the breeding season.

➢ **MANAGEMENT OBJECTIVES:** When planning a breeding schedule, take your management objectives into account. For example, you might decide to breed various groups of does at different times if you want to stagger kidding dates in order to distribute labor and guarantee that children receive individual attention.

THE BEST WAYS TO MAKE A BREEDING SCHEDULE

Think about the following best practices when planning your goat herd's breeding schedule:

Establishing Breeding Groups: Sort your herd into breeding groups according to objectives for breeding, age, and health. By doing this, you can ensure that each group gets the care and attention it need and manage breeding more skillfully.

Track Estrus Cycles: To find out when your does are in heat, monitor their estrus cycles. This might assist you in planning breeding for the best possible time to conceive.

Utilize Breeding Records: Maintain thorough breeding records to monitor mating couples, breeding dates, and other pertinent data. You can use this to keep an eye on the effectiveness of your breeding program and to help you decide what to breed next.

Plan for Kidding: When creating your breeding calendar, take into account the time of kidding. Try to arrange breeding so that the offspring are born when you are ablest to care for them.

An essential component of running a productive goat breeding operation is developing a breeding timetable. You may design a breeding schedule that maximizes the effectiveness of your breeding program and aids in the achievement of your goals for your goat herd by taking into account important variables including the reproductive cycle, breeding season, and management goals. You can also do this by employing proper breeding procedures and best practices.

Assessing the Success of Breeding Programs

To make sure that your herd is healthy, productive, and achieving your management objectives, it is essential to assess the effectiveness of your breeding program. You can find opportunities for improvement and make well-informed decisions to raise the general caliber of your herd by routinely assessing your breeding program. This part will cover critical performance indicators, data analysis, and improvement strategies for assessing the effectiveness of your goat breeding program.

Important Performance Measures for Assessing the Success of Breeding Programs

Reproductive Performance: A crucial determinant of the success of a breeding effort is reproductive performance. Monitor parameters like conception rate, kidding rate, and kidding interval to evaluate your herd's fertility and overall reproductive effectiveness.

Genetic Improvement: Monitor qualities like milk output, growth rate, and conformation to see how your herd has changed genetically over time. Utilize pedigree and performance record data to evaluate your herd's genetic improvement.

Health and illness Management: Keep tabs on key performance indicators for your herd, including as vaccination coverage, death rate, and illness incidence. A thriving breeding program requires a healthy herd.

Production Efficiency: Monitor measures like feed conversion ratio, milk yield per doe, and meat yield per animal to assess your herd's productivity efficiency. Your breeding program can become more profitable and sustainable by increasing production efficiency.

Analyzing Data to Assess the Performance of Breeding Programs

Keeping Records: To aid in data analysis, keep thorough records of breeding, health, and production data. Make use of a system for keeping records that makes it simple to monitor and evaluate key performance metrics.

Data Collection: To guarantee the validity of your analysis, gather data reliably and consistently. When gathering data, follow established procedures to reduce mistakes and guarantee consistency.

Data Interpretation: To effectively analyze your data, use statistical analysis and data visualization approaches. Seek out patterns, trends, and outliers that can shed light on how well your breeding program is working.

Benchmarking: Evaluate your herd's performance in comparison to peers by comparing it to industry norms and benchmarks. Benchmarking can assist you in determining the strengths and weaknesses of your breeding program.

Techniques to Increase the Success of Breeding Programs

Employ Selective Breeding: Enhance your herd's genetic quality by using selective breeding. To maximize your herd's genetic potential, choose breeding stock according to performance metrics, pedigree details, and desired qualities.

Health Management: To keep your herd healthy and prevent sickness, put in place a proactive program for health management. Regularly vaccinate animals, maintain strict biosecurity protocols, and keep an eye out for any symptoms of disease.

Nutrition Management: Make sure the food your goats eat is balanced and satisfies their needs. For optimal reproductive function, milk production, and general health, proper diet is necessary.

Constant Learning: Remain up to date on the most recent advancements in goat management and breeding techniques. Participate in conferences, seminars, and workshops to increase your knowledge and abilities.

Maintaining a healthy and productive herd of goats requires regular evaluation of the breeding program's effectiveness. Enhancing the overall quality and profitability of your breeding program can be achieved through the monitoring of key performance indicators, data analysis, and the implementation of improvement measures. In order to guarantee the long-term viability of your goat herd and assist you accomplish your management objectives, you need regularly assess and modify your breeding program.

GOAT MATING GUIDE   John William Bush (The Farmer's House)

Chapter 10: Breeding Stock Sales & Marketing

Promoting Your Breeding Stock

A successful goat breeding operation requires effective marketing of your breeding stock. You may demonstrate the caliber of your herd, draw in customers, and boost the profitability of your breeding business with the use of efficient marketing techniques. The marketing of your breeding stock will be covered in this chapter along with important tactics, avenues for sales, and successful marketing techniques.

Techniques for Marketing Breeding Stock

1. ESTABLISH A BRAND: Give your breeding business a distinctive brand identity that embodies your principles, standards of quality, and breeding objectives. Having a strong brand will help you stand out from the competition and draw in customers.

2. DISPLAY YOUR HERD: By presenting your breeding stock's genetics, performance information, and conformation, you may draw attention to how high-quality they are. To present your animals and give comprehensive details on their breeding history and pedigree, use high-quality images and videos.

3. TAKE PART IN SHOWS AND EVENTS: To promote your breeding stock and increase brand awareness, take part in goat shows, exhibitions, and other events. Gaining recognition and accolades at events can help your herd's reputation and draw in customers.

4. EMPLOY ONLINE MARKETING: To reach a larger audience of prospective customers, make use of online marketing platforms like social media, websites, and online marketplaces. Post images, videos, and details about your breeding stock to pique curiosity and encourage questions.

5. NETWORKING: To broaden your reach and network, establish connections with other goat breeders, business professionals, and possible purchasers. To network with people in the field, participate in online forums, join associations, and attend industry events.

Outlets for Breeding Stock Sales

1. DIRECT SALES: Through your farm or ranch, sell breeding stock to buyers directly. You may have one-on-one conversations with customers and present your animals in their native habitat when you sell directly to them.

2. ONLINE SALES: To market and sell your breeding stock, use online channels including social media, websites, and online marketplaces. Online sales can expedite transactions and reach a larger pool of prospective customers.

3. AUCTIONS: Sell your breeding stock to the highest bidder by taking part in livestock auctions. A lot of buyers and competitive bidding for your animals can be attracted to auctions.

4. SALES EVENTS: To highlight your breeding stock and draw in purchasers, hold sales events or open houses at your farm or ranch. Sales events have the power to instill in consumers a sense of urgency and enthusiasm.

The Best Ways to Promote and Sell Breeding Stock

1. DELIVER OUTSTANDING CUSTOMER SERVICE: Give purchasers outstanding customer service, which includes quick answers to questions, open communication, and assistance following the sale. Developing rapport and trust with customers can result in recommendations and repeat business.

2. UPHOLD HIGH STANDARDS: To guarantee the caliber of your breeding stock, uphold high standards for animal care, health, and genetics. Purchasing animals who are in good health, have had good care, and have excellent genetics is more likely.

3. INFORM PURCHASERS: Inform purchasers about the advantages of your breeding stock, such as its genetic makeup, track record of performance, and capacity to generate superior offspring. Giving customers advice and information can assist them in making wise choices.

4. RESPECT LEGAL REQUIREMENTS: Make sure you honor all legal obligations when it comes to selling breeding stock, such as health certificates, registration paperwork, and shipping guidelines. Failure to comply may result in legal problems and harm your reputation.

To succeed in the goat breeding business and draw in buyers, you must properly market your breeding stock. You can raise the profile and profitability of your breeding enterprise by building a strong brand, exhibiting your herd, using internet marketing, networking, and employing the appropriate sales channels. You may create a productive and long-lasting breeding program by putting best practices for breeding stock sales and marketing into effect.

Pricing and Sales Negotiation

In the goat business, determining prices and negotiating deals are crucial parts of selling breeding stock. Appropriately pricing your animals and skillfully negotiating sales can help you optimize earnings and guarantee the accomplishment of your breeding business. This chapter will cover pricing techniques for success, negotiating transactions with customers, and setting prices for your breeding stock.

Determining Breeding Stock Prices

1. THINK ABOUT MARKET TRENDS: Find out about local breeding stock prices and market trends in your area. When determining prices, take into account variables like breed, age, genetics, and performance data.

2. ANALYZE YOUR COSTS: Determine how much feed, medical care, and other expenses will cost you while you raise and care for your breeding stock. Make sure your pricing includes a fair profit margin in addition to covering these expenses.

3. EVALUATE GENETICS AND QUALITY: Set your breeding stock price according to its genetic makeup, quality, and likelihood of generating offspring of superior quality. Higher prices can be paid for animals with better genetics and performance records.

4. FACTOR IN DEMAND: When determining prices, take into account the demand for your breeding stock. Genes or breeds that are in great demand can let you charge more, whereas animals in lower demand might need more aggressive pricing.

5. THINK ABOUT YOUR OBJECTIVES: Establish your objectives for selling breeding stock, such as increasing revenue, publicizing your breeding initiative, or decreasing the size of your herd. Your pricing strategy may be influenced by your goals.

Sales negotiations with purchasers

1. BUILD RAPPORT: Be amiable, personable, and informed about your breeding stock to help you build a good rapport with prospective purchasers. Negotiations can go more smoothly and successfully if trust is established.

2. EMPHASIZE BENEFITS: Draw attention to the genetics, performance information, and potential for high-quality offspring that come with your breeding stock. Stress the benefits your animals can provide for the buyer's herd.

3. BE FLEXIBLE: To get to a mutually advantageous deal with the buyer, be prepared to haggle over terms and conditions as well as price. Being adaptable will enable you to seal the deal and cultivate a good rapport with the customer.

4. INFORMATION: Give prospective buyers comprehensive details about your breeding stock, such as medical records, registration documents, and performance metrics. Being open and honest with your animals helps foster confidence and trust.

5. CLOSE THE PURCHASE: As soon as you and the buyer have come to a mutual understanding, proceed to swiftly and expertly close the purchase. Submit the required documentation and make the agreed-upon arrangements for payment and transportation.

Managing Successful Pricing Strategies

Keep an eye on Market Conditions: Be aware of what's going on in the market and modify your price plans accordingly. Pay attention to local pricing for comparable breeding stock as well as trends in supply and demand.

Assess Performance: To make sure your pricing methods are working, assess their performance on a regular basis. To choose the right price, consider profitability, consumer feedback, and sales data.

Provide Incentives: To draw customers and boost sales, think about providing incentives like payment plans, discounts for making numerous purchases, or promotional offers.

Get Input: Find out what customers think about your pricing and sales strategies. Utilize this input to pinpoint areas that need work and, if necessary, modify your pricing methods.

In the goat business, setting prices and negotiating deals are essential components of selling breeding stock. You may increase earnings, draw customers, and guarantee the success of your breeding program by setting prices for your animals fairly, managing pricing strategies for success, and successfully negotiating sales. By putting these tactics into practice, you may accomplish your objectives and create a profitable and long-lasting breeding business.

Sustaining Connections with Purchasers

Sustaining your buyer ties is essential to the long-term viability of your goat breeding enterprise. Developing trusting relationships with customers can result in recommendations, referrals, and repeat business, all of which can help you expand your clientele and improve your standing in the market. The upkeep of buyer relationships will be covered in this chapter, along with communication tactics, customer service procedures, and post-sale assistance.

Techniques of Communication

1. *Remain in Contact:* Use social media, email, or phone conversations to stay in regular contact with your buyers. Inform them about upcoming breeding initiatives, new arrivals, and any exclusive deals or promotions.

2. *Provide Updates:* Provide buyers with information about the animals' progress, including health updates, pregnancy status, and dates of kidding. Giving them regular updates demonstrates your concern for their pets and respect for their company.

3. *Request Feedback:* Find out what customers thought of your customer service and breeding stock. Utilize these comments to pinpoint areas that need work and modify your breeding program.

4. *Be Responsive:* Address questions, worries, and requests from customers as soon as possible. Being receptive demonstrates your awareness of their requirements and dedication to deliver top-notch customer care.

Customer Service Procedures

1. Be Professional: Always conduct yourself with professionalism when interacting with customers. Be mindful of their needs and treat them with courtesy and respect.

2. Give Accurate Information: Make sure the details you give prospective buyers about your breeding stock are correct and current. Information that is false or misleading might harm your credibility and reputation.

3. Offer Assistance: After the sale, offer buyers assistance in the form of resource access, breeding recommendations, and guidance on maintenance and care. Providing assistance can boost customer confidence and foster a sense of program loyalty.

4. Resolve Problems Quickly: Respond to any problems or queries brought up by customers in a timely and courteous manner. Accept responsibility for any errors or issues and collaborate with the customer to come up with a workable solution.

After-Sale Assistance

1. Follow Up: After the sale, get in touch with the purchasers to find out if they are happy with their purchase. Inquire if they have any queries or worries, and extend help if required.

2. Offer Resources: Give purchasers access to resources including breeding advice, care manuals, and contact details for veterinary clinics. By providing resources, sellers can bolster their confidence and sense of support in their abilities to provide for their animals.

3. Offer Promotions or Discounts: As a thank you for their continued business, offer promotions or discounts to loyal customers. This might improve your relationship with customers and promote repeat business.

4. Keep in Touch: Use newsletters, social media, and other avenues of communication to stay in touch with buyers. Continue to add value to their experience as consumers by keeping them updated on new advancements in your breeding program.

Sustaining your buyer relationships is critical to the success of your goat breeding operations. You may develop long-lasting connections with customers that result in repeat business, recommendations, and a favorable reputation in the sector by putting communication strategies, customer service procedures, and post-sale assistance into practice. In the goat breeding business, building relationships with buyers is essential to business growth and long-term success.

GOAT MATING GUIDE   John William Bush (The Farmer's House)

Chapter 11: Legal and Ethical Aspects of Goat Breeding

Welfare of Animals and Breeding Procedures

In order to guarantee the welfare of their animals and adherence to pertinent rules and regulations, goat breeders need to give serious thought to ethical and legal issues. The ethical and legal aspects of goat breeding will be covered in this chapter, along with standards for animal welfare, breeding procedures, and adherence to rules and laws.

Standards for Animal Welfare

1. Provide Sufficient Housing: Make sure your goats have access to hygienic, dry, and cozy quarters that shields them from the weather and offers enough room for them to walk around and rest.

2. Appropriate food: Feed your goats a well-balanced food that takes into account the needs of their age, breed, and reproductive stage. Make sure they always have access to fresh, clean water.

3. Medical Care: Keep a close eye on your goats' health and seek immediate medical attention when necessary. To avoid illness and injury, vaccinate your goats against common diseases and parasites and put in place a health management program.

4. Breeding Procedures: Use responsible breeding techniques by choosing breeding stock according to conformation, genetics, and health. Refrain from breeding animals that have known health problems or genetic flaws.

5. Transport and Handling: Treat your goats with gentleness; try not to put them through needless anxiety or suffering. Make sure their transportation adheres to the best practices for animal transportation and is both safe and compassionate.

Respect for the Laws and Regulations

1. Animal Welfare Laws: Learn about and abide by the local animal welfare laws and rules as they relate to goat breeding. Aspects including housing, care, transportation, and humane euthanasia may be governed by these regulations.

2. Breeding Restrictions: Take note of any local breeding laws pertaining to goats, including those governing registration, breeding, and genetic testing. To stay out of trouble with the law, be sure you abide by these rules.

3. Environmental Regulations: Take into account how your goat breeding business may affect the environment and abide by any rules pertaining to land use, waste management, and conservation techniques.

In order to guarantee the welfare of their animals and adherence to pertinent rules and regulations, goat breeders need to give serious thought to ethical and legal issues. Breeders can improve goat health and welfare and preserve their good name in the business by adhering to rules and regulations, performing responsible breeding, and upholding animal welfare standards.

Regulations Governing the Breeding and Sale of Goats

Depending on the locality, there may be local laws governing animal care, breeding procedures, and sales deals in addition to other criteria for producing and selling goats. To maintain compliance and stay out of trouble with the law, breeders should become aware with these standards. The following are some typical legal prerequisites for raising and selling goats:

REGISTRATION AND LICENSING: In order to breed and sell goats, breeders may be required by some authorities to register their animals or obtain a license.

This could entail applying for a breeding permit from the local government or registering with a breed group.

HEALTH CERTIFICATES: In order to breed and sell goats, breeders may be required to get health certificates attesting to the animals' compliance with health regulations and their absence of contagious diseases.

IDENTIFICATION: For regulatory and traceability reasons, some states mandate that goats wear ear tags or other identifying marks.

SALES CONTRACTS: Breeders may be required to give purchasers a sales contract outlining the conditions of the sale, such as the purchase price, the animal's health state, and any warranties or guarantees, when selling goats.

TRANSPORTATION LAWS: When shipping goats, breeders have to abide by laws pertaining to the safety of the vehicle, the care of the animals during the trip, and the need for certain paperwork.

ZONING AND LAND USE REGULATIONS: Breeders are required to go by any applicable zoning and land use regulations, which may include restrictions on the quantity of animals they may have on their property, the type of housing that must be provided, and the impact on the environment.

ANIMAL WELFARE RULES: Goat care and treatment, including housing, feeding, and veterinary care requirements, are governed by animal welfare rules, which breeders must go by.

LAWS GOVERNING SALES TRANSACTIONS: Breeders are subject to consumer protection laws, which cover things like advertising, product labeling, warranties, and guarantees.

To guarantee compliance and prevent legal problems, breeders must learn about and comprehend the laws that are relevant to their particular area and breeding business.

Breeding Goats' Effects on the Environment

The size of the herd, the management style, and the surrounding environment are some of the variables that might affect how rearing goats affects the environment. While raising goats can have some positive environmental implications, such as offering a sustainable source of dairy and meat, it can also have unfavorable effects if improper management is practiced. The environmental effects of goat breeding will be covered, along with methods for reducing its environmental impact.

LAND USE: Land is needed for housing and grazing when breeding goats. Degradation of pastureland, loss of flora, and soil erosion can result from overgrazing. Goat raising on land can have a minimal negative environmental impact if sustainable land management techniques like pasture enhancement and rotational grazing are implemented.

WATER USE: In order to drink and graze, goats need water. In certain areas, there may be a problem with water scarcity, hence effective water resource management is crucial. Goat breeding's negative environmental effects on water resources can be reduced by putting water conservation measures like effective irrigation and rainwater collection into practice.

WASTE MANAGEMENT: Manure, bedding, and feed leftovers are the waste products of goat raising. Contamination of land and water can result from improper waste management. Composting and appropriate disposal are two waste management techniques that can reduce the environmental impact of goat raising on trash.

GREENHOUSE GAS EMISSIONS: Enteric fermentation and manure management, which produce methane, are the main ways that goat farming can contribute to greenhouse gas emissions. Methane collection systems and nutrition optimization are two examples of sustainable herd management techniques that can assist lower greenhouse gas emissions from goat breeding.

BIODIVERSITY: By grazing on vegetation and posing a competition for resources with native fauna, goat farming can have an impact on biodiversity. Goat rearing can have a minimal negative effect on biodiversity if sustainable grazing techniques are used, such as rotational grazing and habitat protection.

ENERGY USE: The feeding, housing, and transportation of goats during their reproductive process all demand energy. Goat breeding's negative effects on the environment from an energy-use perspective can be mitigated by using renewable energy sources like wind and solar electricity.

Goat breeding can have a large negative influence on the environment, but it can be reduced with sustainable management techniques. Goat breeders can lessen the environmental impact of their operations and advance environmental sustainability by putting into practice strategies like rotational grazing, water saving, waste management, and habitat preservation.

In summary

Benefits and Difficulties of Breeding Goats.

Breeding goats is an interesting but difficult enterprise that presents breeders with a variety of rewards and challenges. This chapter will cover the advantages and difficulties of goat breeding, emphasizing the things that breeders need to know.

Benefits of Breeding Goats:

1. Sustainable Agriculture: By offering a regenerative source of meat, milk, and fiber products, goat rearing supports sustainable agriculture. Goats are an important part of food security and sustainable agriculture because they are effective at converting plants into high-quality protein.

2. Generate Income: Breeders can make money from their goats by selling meat, milk, cheese, and other goat products, as well as breeding stock. Goat rearing may be a lucrative endeavor with the right administration and promotion.

3. *Diversification:* Farmers can increase the variety of agricultural pursuits and revenue sources by breeding goats. Farmers can disperse risk and seize market opportunities in the goat sector by integrating goats into their farming operations.

4. *Environmental Benefits*: Controlled goat grazing has the potential to improve soil fertility, remove weeds, and manage vegetation. Additionally, goats can support sustainable land management techniques like pasture enhancement and rotational grazing.

5. *Cultural and Social Value:* Goats are important to many communities all over the world in terms of both culture and society. Their significance is in their participation in customary rituals, cultural customs, and communal gatherings, which foster togetherness and sense of identity within the group.

Obstacles in Goat Breeding:

1. *Disease Management:* Goats need careful management and veterinary treatment because they are prone to a variety of diseases and health problems. To keep the herd healthy, vaccination campaigns, disease prevention, and biosecurity protocols are crucial.

2. *Predation:* Goat breeders may face serious difficulties due to predation by animals like wolves, coyotes, and dogs. To keep goats safe from predators, proper fencing, guardian animals, and predator deterrents are essential.

3. *Environmental Effects:* Overgrazing, soil erosion, and water pollution are a few of the environmental effects that goat farming may have. To lessen these effects, waste management strategies, conservation initiatives, and sustainable land management techniques are required.

4. *Market Volatility:* Demand, prices, and market circumstances can all fluctuate in the goat market. To effectively navigate the market, breeders need to stay up to date on consumer preferences, pricing variations, and market trends.

5. *Work Intensity:* Raising goats needs constant management, care, and feeding, which can be labor-intensive. It takes time, energy, and money for breeders to properly care for and manage their goat herds.

Goat breeding has several benefits despite its difficulties, such as sustainable agriculture, revenue creation, environmental advantages, and cultural significance. Breeders can create profitable and long-lasting goat breeding enterprises by tackling issues like disease control, predation, environmental effect, market instability, and labor intensity. For breeders worldwide, goat breeding can be a gratifying and rewarding endeavor with the right management, care, and attention.

Closing Remarks and Inspiration

To sum up, growing goats is a lucrative but difficult enterprise that has several advantages for breeders. Goat breeding is essential to community livelihoods, food security, and agricultural sustainability since it generates cash, maintains the environment, and has cultural significance.

As you begin your adventure into goat breeding or as you work to develop and enhance your current breeding program, keep in mind that success demands commitment, tenacity, and never-ending learning. To guarantee your operation's success and longevity, keep up with industry changes, legal regulations, and best practices.

Be resilient, creative, and open to adapting when faced with obstacles including disease control, predators, market instability, and labor intensity. Seek assistance from veterinarians, industry insiders, and other breeders to successfully handle problems and get beyond roadblocks.

Above all, keep in mind that raising goats is a passionate and loving endeavor. Accept the pleasures of raising robust, healthy herds, acknowledging the fruits of successful breeding, and making a positive impact on the long-term viability of agriculture and food production.

Best wishes for your goat-breeding endeavors. I hope your herds grow, your efforts pay off, and you make significant and lasting contributions to the business. Happy equine endeavors!

Appendices

Glossary of Terms

Glossary of terms commonly used in goat mating and breeding

Here is a glossary of terms commonly used in goat mating and breeding:

1. Heat: The period of sexual receptivity in female goats, also known as estrus.

2. Buck: Adult male goat used for breeding.

3. Doe: Adult female goat used for breeding.

4. Kidding: The act of giving birth in goats.

5. Gestation: The period of pregnancy in goats, typically around 150 days.

6. Parturition: The process of giving birth in goats.

7. Colostrum: The first milk produced by the doe after kidding, rich in antibodies.

8. Weaning: The process of separating kids from their mother's milk and transitioning them to solid food.

9. Heat detection: The process of identifying when a female goat is in estrus and ready for breeding.

10. AI (Artificial Insemination): A breeding technique where semen is collected from a male goat and artificially introduced into a female goat's reproductive tract to achieve pregnancy.

11. Estrus synchronization: The process of manipulating the estrus cycle of female goats to ensure they are all in heat at the same time, making breeding more efficient.

12. Flushing: Increasing the nutrient intake of female goats before breeding to improve ovulation rates and fertility.

13. Teaser goat: A male goat used to identify females in heat by exhibiting mating behavior towards them.

14. Line breeding: Breeding closely related goats to maintain or enhance specific traits.

15. Outcrossing: Breeding goats from unrelated lines to introduce new genetic material.

16. Inbreeding: Breeding goats that are closely related, which can lead to genetic defects.

17. Selective breeding: Breeding goats with desirable traits to perpetuate those traits in future generations.

18. Purebred: A goat that belongs to a recognized breed and has a documented pedigree.

19. Crossbreed: A goat resulting from the mating of two different breeds.

20. Homozygous: Having identical alleles for a particular gene.

21. Heterozygous: Having different alleles for a particular gene.

22. Heritability: The degree to which a trait is passed down from parents to offspring.

23. Recessive gene: A gene that is only expressed when an individual has two copies of it.

24. Dominant gene: A gene that is expressed when an individual has at least one copy of it.

25. Genotype: The genetic makeup of an individual.

26. Phenotype: The observable characteristics of an individual, which are determined by both genetic and environmental factors.

27. Embryo transfer: A reproductive technique where embryos are collected from a donor female goat and transferred to recipient female goats to achieve pregnancy.

28. Buck effect: The phenomenon where the presence of a male goat stimulates estrus in female goats.

29. Polled: Goats without horns, either naturally or through a genetic trait.

30. Freemartin: A sterile female calf born twin to a male calf due to hormonal influences from the male twin.

31. Scrapie: A fatal, degenerative disease affecting the nervous system of sheep and goats.

32. Caprine Arthritis Encephalitis (CAE): A viral disease affecting goats, characterized by arthritis and encephalitis.

This glossary provides a basic overview of key terms related to goat mating and breeding. It is important to consult additional resources and experts for more detailed information on specific topics.

Sample Breeding Records

Here is a sample breeding record template that you can use to track breeding information for your goats:

Breeding Record for Goat Herd

Date: _____

Goat ID: _____

Breed: _____

Sex: _____

Date of Birth: _____

Sire: _____

GOAT MATING GUIDE   John William Bush (The Farmer's House)

Dam: _____

Breeding Date: _____

Expected Due Date: _____

Pregnancy   Confirmed   (Yes/No):
_____

Notes: _____

Date of Birth: _____

Number of Kids: _____

Kid ID: _____

Sex: _____

Birth Weight: _____

Notes: _____

Health Status: _____

You can customize this template to include any additional information that is relevant to your breeding program, such as vaccination records, health status, or any other details you want to track for each goat. Keeping detailed breeding records can help you track the breeding history of your goats, monitor their reproductive health, and make informed breeding decisions.

www.ingramcontent.com/pod-product-compliance
Lightning Source LLC
Chambersburg PA
CBHW052158220526
45471CB00004B/1729